The Yin and Yang of BodyBuilding

AUTOTONICS

a system for the
Ultimate Exercise Machine

Dr. James Farnham

 Aardvark Books, Hibbing, Minn.

The Yin and Yang of Bodybuilding

AUTOTONICS

a system for the
Ultimate Exercise Machine

by: Dr. James Farnham

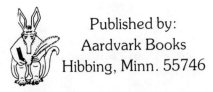

Published by:
Aardvark Books
Hibbing, Minn. 55746

All rights reserved including the right
to reproduce this book or portions
thereof in any form.

Copyright © 1986 by Dr. James Farnham
First printing 1986

ISBN 0-936619-17-1

To Jay and Jesse, my sons,
whose mere presence could
inspire anyone to do any-
thing.

Jim Farnham

CONTENTS

Warning - Disclaimer

The ideas expressed in this book are based on the author's ongoing thirty years experience in physical fitness. The exercises were designed by utilizing applied kinesiology and are to the author's knowledge unique in form, although, they may be similar in concept to other exercises. If they resemble other exercises in form it is unintentional and purely coincidental.

Because of the unlimited differences in genetic makeup, motivation, performance, nutrition and other factors, gains in body tone, body size, and strength can also be extremely variable.

The author and publisher disavow any injury that could result, or allegedly result, from the performance of these exercises. The exercises herein are relatively safe when done properly, but as with any exercise program injuries are possible. Participants should be aware of this and engage in them at their own discretion.

Warning - Disclaimer

About the cover:

I feel that the principles underlying Autotonics embody the idea of the Yin and Yang, inasmuch as they emphasize the positive and negative aspects of the muscle contractions as equal components of the movement. The Eastern philosophy emphasizes the importance of the mind-body connection; this same idea is emphasized in Autotonics. It is for this reason that I chose the Yin Yang symbol to represent the cover illustration. The corona of the sun emerging from behind the symbol is meant to convey the birth of a new and innovative approach to exercising. Since there is no machine as unique and complicated as the human machine, I feel justified in calling it the "ultimate exercise machine."

Autotonics certainly fits the criteria, better than any other exercise system, to be called the Yin and Yang of bodybuilding, a system for the ultimate exercise machine.

Acknowledgments:

In any endeavor, there are many people who, by their encourage-ment and positive attitude, keep you striving forward. I would like tc thank all my positive strokers.

I would like to thank my children for the "dad time" they sacrificec while their dad's attention was diverted by this project.

I want to thank my wife, Gail, for proofreading and offering suggestions on the developing manuscript. She also served as my model while I laboriously tried to graphically depict the exercises Heaped with these duties, she still patiently tried the various exercises reporting her opinion on their effectiveness. And on top of all this, she extended me the same sabbatical my children did as I isolated m; mind and spirit in this undertaking.

Mary Ann Lund merits a well-deserved "E" for effort for accepting my handwritten scribble sheets and deciphering them into a workable typewritten rough draft.

Photographers get many strange assignments, but I must thank Mike Stehlin for his unwavering composure at my male "beefcake request.

My special thanks goes to George Peterson, my friend, and former mentor, who reacquainted me with the subtleties of grammar punctuation, and sentence structure (not to mention spelling). He smoothed off the rough edges and filled in the holes of my manu script, and if that weren't enough to ask of a friend, he typed it into a presentable form. This task would be enough for a person who has nothing else to do, but he found time for this project among the items in his otherwise busy schedule, and I am humbly grateful.

J.

Preface

I was born in the early Forties, when the world was in a great turmoil, and I can only infer that the pressures on that generation preempted just about any thoughts but those of survival and reversing chaotic events back to some kind of sanity.

After the war, rebuilding began on a worldwide scale. America was too busy to think beyond the reconstruction of a normal society: homes to build, families to build, and lives to rebuild.

Growing up during this era, I was oblivious to what had happened. Then, around 1955, when certain noticeable and curious phenomena were starting to happen to my mind and body, something unique began to happen in America—Rock and Roll. That magnetic, unifying force suddenly gave the youth of this country an identity, and like it or not, an era had started. Rock and Roll swept the country, invaded our homes, and, I'm sure, gave parents not only a reason to forget the horror they had lived through but also a reason to concentrate on a new "horror," certainly innocuous by comparison, but a force that nevertheless had to be reckoned with. Unfortunately, it was too much for them. Rock and Roll prevailed, and in spite of it we teenagers survived intact.

Now, it seems to me, such eras explode on us about every ten years or so. An emerging class of young people, preoccupied with Rock and Roll, suddenly became aware of a bigger world around them and developed a social consciousness that grabbed America by its very bowels and attempted to turn it inside out. The profoundness of it all was too much to handle without the use of an extraneous source of mind-adjusting drugs, either to escape reality or to focus on it.

In spite of this gut wrenching catharsis, America held together, proving that the principles underlying our society are stronger than the problems overlying it.

The turbulent Sixties gave way to a host of unanswered questions and troubled minds, an era of introspection began: "Who are we? Who am I? Where are we going? Where am I going?" and searching questions of similar nature. We explored our psyches in all conceivable ways: group therapy, retreats, E.S.T., encounter groups, and a plethora of self-help manuals. America's minds were in trouble.

We focused on our heads, and this spread to our feet, and we began to run, first for our wellbeing and then for our very lives. After we started to run, the pain in our feet helped to make us forget the pain in our brain, but it gave us something new to worry about. All the material in between! Were we too fat? Too skinny? Eating right? We began asking questions, and the answers seemed to be making sense; consequently, a new era is overtaking us—the Body Consciousness Era.

I believe we are starting to understand that we are actually *connected* from our head to our feet. Our minds help our bodies, and our bodies help our minds. The foods we eat, the water we drink, and the air we breathe all have a large impact on this machine that we are housed in.

As we approach the Body Consciousness Era or, more accurately, move further into it, we are being bombarded with devices of compelling ingenuity to aid us in building the body of our dreams. Barbells and dumbbells, cables and springs suddenly don't seem to be enough. Machines are being invented that allow injury-free, controlled-resistance movements. They employ cams and cables, cables and weight stacks, weight stacks and levers, hydraulics, compressed air, water, and now, of course computerized resistance and digital readouts. You have to be a very wealthy person or belong to a gym to take advantage of all these wonderful contrivances that you push and pull on your way to a shapely, healthy body.

What all these machines and extraneous devices really do, in the final analysis, is provide resistance against which your muscles work. The resistance is structured so that is works the muscles through their normal anatomic function.

It seems to me, as an observer of eras, that in our search for the ultimate machine, we have forgotten the oldest and most wonderful one of all—ourselves! This is what Autotonics is all about. Before this era of body consciousness loses itself in an infinite variety of machines, devices, and confusion, we must tie the circle, and Autotonics does just that. Read the ensuing chapters and let Autotonics re-introduce you to your best friend—you—and as each of us becomes conscious of our body connections, perhaps this will be the era in which we're able to tie in all of the other bodies and minds in our world, and health will become contagious.

J.F.

THE JOURNEY OF

A THOUSAND MILES

BEGINS WITH

THE FIRST STEP

Lao Tsu

PART ONE

AUTOTONICS: THE BIRTH OF A SYSTEM

THE TEN THOUSAND THINGS CARRY YIN AND EMBRACE YANG THEY ACHIEVE HARMONY BY COMBINING THESE FORCES

FROM: TAO TE CHING

Chapter One

Necessity: The Mother of Autotonics

Bodybuilding—the term conjures up images of musclebound men and women in narcissistic poses, shaved clean and glistening with oil, their suntanned bodies twisted into contorted figures of severely accentuated muscle bound with cords of taut blood vessels. Originally, this may have been the ultimate goal or the direction bodybuilding led to for only a selected group of genetically gifted individuals, but as has happened in other sports, there is now also a definite movement to incorporate the rest of society into this phenomenon.

Bodybuilding's image is beginning to change, or at least to be recognized as including all aspects of health and fitness, and in all the literature that abounds today, there is no greater purveyor of that image than Joe Weider and his publication, *Muscle and Fitness Magazine*.

Bodybuilding is for everyone, and a new definition is emerging. Bodybuilding is now a method used not only to build the body with respect to the size and shape of its muscles, but also to improve nutritional, physiological, and character development. These are also the goals I have intended for Autotonics.

The name "Autotonics" is derived from "auto", meaning "self", and "tonic", meaning "building a healthy muscular condition as well as restoring physical and mental tone."

The concepts behind Autotonics are as old as the days when athletes began engaging in physical competition and looking for means to increase their strength, but the idea of systematizing the concepts and organizing them into a valid, workable exercise program is new. Autotonics utilizes the muscles of the body to provide resistance exercises that simulate free weights and apparatus. Autotonics elevates a few hackneyed movements and introduces a collection of new exercises into a powerful, legitimate system of body-building, taking advantage of modern body building techniques to enhance the efficiency of the exercises.

I have personally trained with weights for twenty-eight years and have utilized them in various ways. In my early years I lifted weights to improve my strength and size, which I accomplished; but without any system to follow, my gains were limited, and my interest waned. I used weight training to improve my strength for other sports and also for competitive powerlifting later on. Although my interest waxed and waned, I never really lost touch with weight training.

In the past few years my interest has been rekindled by body-building. I must admit that I had always had a negative image of the sport, but after reading a copy of *Muscle and Fitness Magazine*, I began to change that image. I could see that bodybuilders had tremendous overall strength, flexibility, and agility. This new image gained my attention on television, in the *Super-stars Competition*, and in the *Strongest Man Competition* series.

New methods were being introduced, or perhaps revealed, to the general public, as I myself was unaware of them in all my previous years of weight training. High intensity training, with clear instructions on deriving the most from your efforts, was being introduced. This era of new bodybuilding was beginning to emerge into public view and, having the tendency to become obsessed with things, I indulged.

I felt that in order to stimulate myself to the greatest efforts, I would compete in some contests—which I have—and for me this was a great learning experience. One of the things obsession tends to forge is the mettle of a person, and competition hones it. For me, in the case of bodybuilding, it meant not wanting to miss a workout. There are times when, because of meetings, vacation, and so on, you must interrupt your training. I tried on these occasions to compensate by using portable apparatus or going to local gyms to work out, but this never seemed to fill the void.

The adage is that necessity is the mother of invention, and the necessity to fill that void led me to begin experimenting with body movements that I had toyed with off and on for twenty-five years, but had never given serious attention. By applying knowledge about anatomical function which I had gained in my training as a Doctor of Veterinary Medicine and coupling it with my new interest, body-building, I started to fabricate a series of exercises I could use while traveling. The exercises worked so well and duplicated so well the weight training methods I was using that I decided to organize them into the system I call Autotonics. The more I worked with the exercises, the more convinced I became that this exercise program was for everyone.

Chapter Two

Yin and Yang of Bodybuilding

At first glance you might think that this book is about some ancient Eastern exercise system, because the exercises are as ancient as our own anatomy. The system, however, is based on totally modern bodybuilding methods.

According to the Chinese, the "Tao" is the ultimate or underlying reality, and the "Yin" and "Yang" represent the opposite poles of our concepts of reality, the positive and negative aspects of all phenomena. They are opposite but inseparable; where one ends the other begins, and neither is ultimate but contains an element of each within the other. The "Chi" represents the energy within the universe, the life force, and this energy ties the Yin and Yang together.

One way of looking at this would be to use, as a crude model, a flashlight and a battery. The light is our conceptual reality of an invisible force, the Chi, or current. The negative and positive poles of the battery, the Yin and Yang, are distinct and opposite entities, but still an equal and inseparable part of the current.

The Chinese philosophers believe that our bodies are a microcosm of the Universe and, in fact, base their acupuncture techniques on the Yin and Yang flow of energy as it circulates within the body. The martial arts, especially *Akido* and *Tai Chi Chuan*, develop the flow of the Chi energy. Demonstrations of this power are awesome. In fact, the energy within our body is awesome, as the ancients knew, and as the great scientist Albert Einstein proved with his formula $E = MC^2$. The potential energy, for instance, within a gram of matter (A fingernail weighs about a gram) is roughly equivalent to the explosion of a thousand tons of TNT. Einstein's theory led the way to the development of the atom bomb, demonstrating the energy that exists in matter.

What, then, does Chinese philosophy have to do with Autotonics?

Autotonics embodies the principle of the Yin and Yang because it utilizes the positive and negative contractions of our muscles and because it uses our bodies as the resistance force. Consequently, the energy flow stays within the body and isn't expended into an extraneous piece of equipment. When I work out with Autotonics, I like to feel the Chi flowing into the muscles. With each positive and negative movement I feel the Yin and Yang energies concentrating the Chi, providing both a psychological uniting of the mind and body and a diversion from the mechanical aspect involved in doing repetitions of the exercises.

The Yin (negative) and Yang (positive) forces are used in resisting and contracting forces throughout Autotonics workouts. As you feel these forces and feel the Chi flowing into the muscles being worked, you will enhance your workout in a special way that elevates Autotonics above other types of exercise systems. Concentration is a key element in bodybuilding, and concentrating on your life force (Chi) is the best way to derive the utmost benefit from Autotonics, the Yin and Yang of bodybuilding.

Chapter Three

The Who and the Why

Autotonics is for everyone, as I stated earlier, although everyone may not think so. Let me explain.

First, to the "hard core" bodybuilders, as I suspect they would be the most resistant to employ Autotonics, because once the "iron bug" has bitten, pumping iron becomes an almost unparalleled obsession. I merely want to invite iron pumpers to try this method, as I did while traveling and vacationing, because the proof of Autotonics is in the using. Also, Autotonics can be utilized in the iron game at the end of an exercise for "forced reps" if no partner is available; as "burns," if done rapidly at the end of a weight movement; and at the end of a workout for a pumping movement. Autotonics can also be employed as a pre-exhaustion movement with weight training. Autotonics provides an excellent way to pump up for contest or camera. Without question, Autotonic exercises can be intergrated with weight training without compromising the ideals of either method.

Autotonics can be used by anyone involved in any sport who wishes to concentrate on weak points. For the average "spectator," seeking to enhance strength and shape, Autotonics has many definite advantages. Because they are inherently progressive, Autotonic exercises are far more productive than calisthenics. Calisthenic movements use body resistance in various forms that are only progressive in the number of repetitions, which are usually limited by either aerobic exhaustion or boredom, whichever comes first. Autotonics employs body resistance also, but the progression is inherent in the exercise. Consider the basis for weight training, or machine training, or any type of apparatus training. The basis for each is to provide resistance against which your muscle works. The principle is to keep increasing the resistance at various intervals so that the muscle is forced to grow bigger and stronger to compensate for the increased demands on it. That is the same principle employed in Autotonics. For instance, the curl in Autotonics used to build the biceps and bracialis muscles uses the triceps and shoulder muscles of the opposite arm to provide resistance. The biceps and bracialis respond to the resistance by growing in size and strength; correspondingly, the triceps and deltoid muscles of the opposite arm grow. The next time you perform the exercise, the resistance increases by a corresponding amount. The transition is smoother than with barbells or machines, because the increase in resistance keeps pace with the opposing muscles. Besides providing progressive resistance, Autotonics provides variable resistance better than any machine could possibly do. Variable resistance means that the amount of resistance applied is varied over the range of movement of the exercise. For instance, if you were doing a curl movement with a barbell, the start of the movement would be relatively easy, but as the arm started moving in an arc, you would hit a point where the movement would be at its weakest mechanical point, called the "sticking point," approximately where the elbow is at ninety degrees. After you pass this point, the movement becomes easier again. Obviously, the amount of weight you can handle in any given exercise is determined by the amount of weight you can handle at the sticking point. Some machines are supposedly designed to compensate for that by providing more resistance when your strength in the movement is greater and less resistance at the sticking point, so that you can theoretically use maximum force throughout the movement. No machine accomplishes this better than your own body through Autotonics. With Autotonics, you employ one hundred percent resistance at all points of the movement. Your computer brain directs your machine muscle to provide the correct resistance throughout the movement with precision unattainable when using any mechanical apparatus.

I don't want to imply that Autotonics is superior to weight training in building muscle. Some of the most muscular men and women in the world have been developed by weight training methods. The only way to compare the two methods would be by scientific experiments using controlled groups equal in body type, nutrition, and motivation. However, just as weight training has certain advantages, so does Autotonics.

Safety is one big advantage of Autotonics. I have sustained many injuries in weight training; e.g., a broken toe from dropping a weight, a sprained back from using too much weight in squats, muscle tears, sprains, and bruises of various kinds. Any time you start swinging iron around, you are open to some kind of injury. Machines offer some advantages in safety over free weights, but Autotonics offers the ultimate in safety. There is nothing to drop, and since the resistance is tailored for each person, by himself, overextension is almost impossible.

Cost, or the lack of cost, is another substantial advantage. Purchasing machines is out of the question for persons of average means. The cost of barbells and dumbbells is nominal, but in order to do a full range of bodybuilding movements, you have to start purchasing adjunctive apparatus, at which point cost starts to approach that of machines. Joining a gym is becoming increasingly and, for some, prohibitively expensive. The purchase price of this book, on the other hand, provides you with a lifetime membership *in your own gym.*

Less time involvement is a definite advantage, especially if you would have to travel very far to a workout center. The time getting prepared to go, and the transportation to and from, often involve as much or more time as the workout itself.

Privacy is an advantage with Autotonics. If you don't like feeling self-conscious around a gym or machine club, use Autotonics in the privacy of your own home, with the mirror as your only critic.

A very considerable advantage of Autotonics is that you don't have to lose continuity of workouts, because once you learn the methods and principles, you always have a complete gym with you wherever you are.

Autotonics spans both gender and age gaps. Because you control the amount of resistance, you are capable of finding your own starting point. You can apply as much resistance as only you are capable of; therefore, each exercise is uniquely personal. Autotonics can be employed by the very young and the very old, even by the physically handicapped. People confined to wheelchairs, for example, can use Autotonics whereas using free weights or apparatus could be unwieldy and potentially dangerous.

I would like to add here a note of caution. Autotonics, if done properly, is very physically demanding, and although it can be done by anyone, users should take the same precautions (as you would before engaging in any physical fitness program) of having a complete physical exam and discussing their intentions with their doctor.

To recapitulate, Autotonics provides a system of exercise that spans the entire spectrum of age, sex, and body type. It can be used as a total physical fitness, bodybuilding, conditioning, or strengthening system, or as ancillary exercise for certain sports to improve athletic ability. Autotonics is inexpensive, psychologically and physically rewarding, and the most versatile form of exercise available now and for the rest of your life.

IT IS MORE
IMPORTANT
TO SEE THE
SIMPLICITY
TO REALIZE ONE'S
TRUE NATURE

FROM: TAO TE CHING

PART TWO

THE "ERN" FORMULA
EXERCISE
RECUPERATION
NUTRITION

KNOWING

IGNORANCE IS

STRENGTH

IGNORING

KNOWLEDGE IS

SICKNESS

FROM: TAO TE CHING

Chapter Four

Some Can, But Everyone Can Try

Before describing the specific exercises of Autotonics, there are some important principles that should be addressed if we expect to achieve our goals: increased strength, better health, and a more esthetically pleasing physique.

First, let us consider genetics, the specific protein codes that give us our individual characteristics; e.g., hair color, eye color, height, and body type. These codes determine much of our athletic ability, mental ability, personality, and even our susceptibility to certain diseases. Some genetic characteristics are obviously unchangeable, but most are alterable to some degree. To be realistic is to understand that two people placed in the same situation, with equal control over the variables of diet, sleep, and training, will probably progress at different rates, because of genetics.

The reason I am pointing this out is that although Autotonics is as fine an exercise program as anyone can follow, it is not the magic elixir that will transform you into an overnight Venus or Adonis. The most practical and ideal goal to strive for is to improve yourself to the utmost of your own genetic limits, not only physically, but mentally and emotionally as well.

Now that we have disposed of what we have little control over, let's explore other factors necessary for progress in reaching our goals through Autotonics.

Chapter Five

Necessary Stress

"Stress" is a loosely used present-day term with a generally accepted negative connotation. Stress is a collective term used to denote excesses, inadequacies, and dissatisfactions in our work, social and economic endeavors. These examples represent some emotional stresses, but stress can also arise from physical causes such as environmental sources of heat, cold, noise, thirst, hunger, injuries, and infections. All living things are constantly bombarded by different stresses. It is not the number of stresses that is the most important consideration, but how we are able to adapt to stress. In wild animals and primitive societies, survival depends on the individual's ability to adapt (the survival of the fittest). Stress is actually nature's way of strengthening living things.

In modern, civilized society we have been able to lessen environmental stress, but even though life is more comfortable, the result of modern civilization is a weaker mankind. The increase in technology decreases the amount of physical work that is required to survive, which leads to a more sedentary existence and makes us more vulnerable and less adaptable to environmental stress. As diets become more refined and unnatural, we become more prone to nutritional stress and infectious stress. To fight back, modern man creates drugs to combat these enemies. As our work environments become noisy, crowded, competitive, and callous, emotional stress is inevitable. To fight back, modern man creates more drugs to combat these enemies. We constantly look for the "quick fix" for our problems, but for the true answers we must look to the past, to the strengths of our ancestors. We must learn to combat stress by strengthening our bodies and minds. We can't continue to avoid stress by creating newer, more powerful drugs as crutches. A more logical way to fight back is to utilize the principles of good nutrition and regular exercise. To enhance our enjoyment of the wonderful modern conveniences we have created, we have to become "selectively primitive" again, learning to take advantage of necessary stress.

I would like to define "stress" as a "disruption of equilibrium that results in an adaptive change." If adaption takes place, the organism is strengthened and is able to withstand the same stress next time without disruption of the equilibrium. If the stress is too intense or prolonged, and the organism is unable to adapt, deleterious effects are the consequence.

By applying the stress/adaption principles to exercise, we can increase muscle size, improve metabolism, and become physically stronger. This is important because we can overcome daily stresses more easily. Looking back at some of the examples of stress that I have mentioned, you can see that learning how to adapt is the key to emotional and physical survival and happiness.

If we provide necessary stress in the form of controlled exercise, at regular intervals, with progressive increments, allowing time for adaption to occur, muscle growth and strength will follow. At first your muscles will respond rapidly, with fast increases. As you progress, the amount of stress (exercise) needed for additional progress will also increase, and your gains will plateau—discouragement is common at this point, and specialized stress/adaption techniques will be needed to achieve new muscle gains (these techniques will be explained in later chapters). We must be careful during plateau periods not to turn productive stress against us by overexercising and overcoming our capability to adapt.

Autotonics is the perfect stress/adaption system for muscle growth and general health improvement. Autotonics provides a large variety of movements that exercise all body parts. It provides the physical stress in just the right increments to cause and allow adaption. It provides a psychological approach to allow adaption to emotional stress. Autotonics provides all the properties that an exercise system needs for necessary stress.

Chapter Six

The "Rest" of the Story

A trap that almost everyone who starts any type of exercise program falls into is "the more the better." While it is true that the harder you stress a muscle the faster and bigger it will grow, it is also true that a rest period must follow to allow the body to rebuild the now-injured muscle cells. In the rebuilding process, the body not only repairs the muscles cells but reinforces them, adding new tissue, thus increasing the size and strength.

This brings us to the second criterion of muscle growth, equally as important, *recuperation*. As a muscle is strongly exercised and stressed, it is essential that a period of rest should follow, usually forty-eight hours for most people although some highly advanced athletes have developed more recuperative powers after many years of training. For beginners and intermediates, three days a week seems to work out best, for both a recuperative and a social schedule.

Chapter Seven

Getting to the Meat of Nutrition

The first two criteria of the "ERN" Formula, exercise and recuper
ation, are immensely dependent upon the third criterion, *nutrition*
The body must be adequately and properly nourished if optimum
growth is to take place.

I have read so many articles on nutrition by so many expert
with so many differing views that I almost hesitate to get into i
discussion of "proper nutrition." Nevertheless, I have to mentior
some general, rational attitudes toward the subject because, even
though confusing, it is essential: without good nutrition, you won't b
able to reach your full potential with Autotonics (or any other system
of exercise).

Try to eat "balanced meals," meals that contain foods from th
basic food groups such as meats, grains, vegetables, fruits, milk, an
eggs. (If you are a vegetarian, you are already aware of the necessit
of balancing foods for ultimate nutrition.) These foods should b
eaten sometime within the day, everyday. Meals should be eaten i
smaller portions five to six times a day, instead of the convention
three meals a day.

Avoid highly refined foods, which usually contain excess fat an
"empty calories," devoid of the micronutrients such as vitamins an
minerals necessary for their proper metabolism. Highly refined foo
also contain simple sugars that are absorbed rapidly and converte
to glucose, causing sharp increases in insulin release, usually ove
shooting the actual need. This in turn leads to hypoglycemia. Firs
you experience a satisfied "high," so to speak, where the organ
especially the brain, are satiated. This is abruptly followed by a peric
when the organs are left hungry, leading to the hypoglycem
reactions of irritability, inability to concentrate, and tiredness. It
better to ingest more complex carbohydrates that are broken dow

and absorbed slower, avoiding the insulin peaks and valleys. Eating more often also keeps insulin release at a lower level. Excess insulin promotes the storage of fat, can contribute to atherosclerosis, and inhibits growth hormone release from the anterior pituitary; growth hormone which is essential for building muscle as well as keeping our immune system strong for fighting off diseases.

Generally speaking, the "closer to the earth" we eat, the better our nutrition will be. By that, I mean the less cooking of foods, the more nutritious they are. Vegetables should be eaten raw if possible, or steamed instead of boiled. If boiled, the water should be added back into the meal in gravies or sauces. Try to start with fresh vegetables and fruit, since canning and freezing destroys most of the vitamins. Meats should be baked or broiled, as frying tends to break down protein and the fats are absorbed in the meat. Eat sensibly, eat slowly, give your body a little time to assimilate the food it ingests. Chances are that if you leave the table a little hungry, in about fifteen minutes to a half hour, when your food is absorbing and your blood sugar begins to rise, the feeling of hunger will disappear.

To summarize, balance your meals, avoid highly refined foods, eat smaller meals more often, eat closer to the earth, eat slower, and give your meals a chance to digest.

Supplements—the controversy rages on. Living as we do in a society that processes its foods more, and has added uncountable chemical pollutants to the environment, we find that our meals alone, even though seemingly well balanced, may not provide enough micronutrients to keep us at optimum health. Not only in my opinion, but borne out by scientific experiments, supplements are necessary. B vitamins are utilized mainly as co-enzymes in metabolism and are necessary for proper nerve and brain functions. Vitamins C and E are important antioxidants, protecting cells from destruction of the internally produced and externally ingested pollutants. The only vitamins that have toxic properties when ingested to excess are A, D, and K, and prudence should prevail with their use.

I also believe that a balanced mineral supplement is judicious. I stated the "controversy rages," and I suggest reading further on the subject if you feel uncomfortable with my suggestions.

Another controversial subject related to nutrition and bodybuilding is the amount of protein we should eat while exercising. Generally, it has been shown through observation that hard training athletes require a higher protein level to maintain themselves. One area that shows protein depletion is the decreased red blood cell production and manufacture of hemaglobin with a resulting marginal anemia called "athletic anemia." Bodybuilders over the years have generally eaten more protein because they have observed the results. Remember to take increased supplements of Vitamin B_6, with higher protein intake to help metabolize it properly, and if you're over forty, betaine HCL taken with a protein meal helps to digest and break down the proteins into amino acids so they can be assimilated.

While on the subject of nutrition and exercise, let me make quite clear that Autotonics alone will not cause weight gain or loss. To lose a pound of fat takes a deficit of 3500 calories. To acccomplish this by exercise alone is a prodigious feat: jogging burns approximately six hundred calories per hour, so to lose a pound of fat you would have to run about six hours. Simply not eating for a day would accomplish approximately the same thing. The point is that it is much easier to lose weight by cutting down on your caloric intake than by increasing your caloric output through hours of aerobic exercise. This is not meant to discount aerobics, because I believe that some form of aerobics provides a healthy balance for any exercise program.

The best exercise for weight loss that I know of is the "two-hand push." As natural inclinations start to overtake reason at the supper table, place one hand on either side of your plate and firmly push yourself into a standing position!

These three chapters have given you the basic formula for success, the ERN Formula: Exercise, Recuperation, and Nutrition. In the exercise game, you earn what you get, and you get what you ERN.

PART THREE

THE EXERCISES

YIELD AND

OVERCOME

BEND AND BE

STRAIGHT

EMPTY AND BE FULL

WEAR OUT AND

BE NEW.

FROM: TAO TE CHING

Chapter Eight

Autotonics: Progressive Resistance Without Apparatus

This chapter concludes with a list of fifty exercises that compose the Autotonics system. At first glance they may appear to be just a conglomeration of every possible way to push or pull your body. Let me assure you that every exercise has been carefully designed, utilizing kinesiology and that the performance of each is based on the anatomic function of the "target muscle group." What I mean by the target muscle group is the muscle intended to be exercised. Even though you use an opposing muscle or muscle group to provide resistance, the resistor muscle functions at an anatomic advantage, so the main focus is on the target muscle. The opposing muscle group, by participating, does derive some benefit, and because of this, two advantages are inherent: first, the principle of progressive resistance is created, and second, combination exercises can be created that work opposing muscle groups, as will be explained after we have gone through the exercises themselves.

You will find that there are several exercises for each muscle group. The reasons for this are threefold. First multiple exercises provide alternative movements that may in some respects be easier to perform which can be helpful for persons who have a handicap that inhibits certain ranges of movement. Ease and variety of performance also allows all users to adapt more comfortably to the program and to find their own comfort range. Second, having enough exercises to change programs helps to decrease boredom. Third, the exercises work the muscles from different aspects of their anatomic function. For example, the large muscles of the chest, the pectoralis major muscles, perform several different functions. They flex the shoulder joint, they help to rotate the humerus, or upper arm bone, medially (twist it toward the front of the body), and they assist in pulling the arm toward the center of the body or adducting the arm.

37

Contributing to the mass of the chest, the pectoralis minor and serratus muscles pull the shoulder forward. Two of the Autotonics chest exercises utilize these anatomic functions in the following manner.

In the Pec Push, the chest muscles perform their function of flexing the shoulder, and at the end of the movement the shoulder is brought forward, activating the pectoralis minor muscle (the small chest muscle lying under the larger ones) and serratus muscles.

The Low Pec Push utilizes the pectoralis muscle in a different way, employing the other anatomic functions of the muscle. First, because of the way the hands are placed, the arms are rotated medially and second, in the way the arms are moved during the exercise, the arm is adducted.

Using these two chest exercise movements, therefore, works the muscle by utilizing four of its anatomic functions, thus building the muscle more fully and making it more shapely. This theme of varying anatomic functions has been carried throughout the design of the Autotonics exercise program.

If the exercises resemble, at times, those used by weight trainers or machine oriented training, the reason is more than coincidental. The use of weights and the design of exercise equipment is based on the anatomical function of the muscles, as Autotonics is. Just as different variations of an exercise are used in weight training to work different muscles, so this principle is applied with Autotonics. For example, with the barbell bench press, if your grip on the bar is very wide, you put most of the stress on the pectoralis muscles; with a medium range grip you bring the anterior deltoids, triceps, and pectoralis muscles all into play at the same time; and with a very narrow grip you stress the triceps more. Autotonics uses the same principle in the Bent Press with a wide, medium, and narrow stance of the legs.

As you study the different exercises, you will see the legitimacy of their design. The fact that you are using resistance through your own body makes them resistance movements, and because they are inherently progressive, this makes Autotonics a progressive resistance exercise program.

Autotonics involves a bit of imagination and practice, especially dealing with mind-muscle control. You must concentrate with each movement to obtain the desired resistance and results. Don't be easy on yourself, develop self-discipline, because only through one hundred percent effort will you obtain the greatest benefits. If you cheat on the resistance, you cheat only yourself.

A note of caution and advice should be interjected here. As you begin the routines or experiment with the individual exercises, it is better to use less that one hundred percent effort for several reasons. Number one, if you haven't warmed up properly, the "cold" muscle has a greater probability of injury. Two, these exercises take practice to get the proper "feel" for the movement, and using less resistance to begin with will allow the correct mind/muscle correlation. Third, is common to start exercising too hard in the beginning which tends to injure muscles, leaving them sore. This only causes frustration. Autotonics should be fun and productive, not frustrating. Only after you are comfortable with the exercises, and have decided on your goals with the program, should you go for broke.

The following pages describe the exercises in detail and then give suggestions on exercise routines. The exercises are described starting from the head down, and divisions have been made for the various muscle groups. Some exercises may overlap and may be included in more than one group; in these instances the overlap will be noted, and the exercise will not be counted as a separate exercise.

Chapter Nine

Neck

The neck plays its most important role in certain sports, such as wrestling and boxing. In wrestling, the neck acts like another appendage to lift and turn the body in various situations for both offense and defense. In boxing, the strength of the neck is extremely important in protecting against a knockout blow. In bodybuilding the neck comes into importance for balancing the esthetics of the body. A set of wide shoulders is descredited by a pencil neck sitting on top of and between them. The neck should be thick without becoming exaggerated. The trapezius muscles should be prominent at the back of the neck to give the base a heavier look, with the whole effect being a tapered flow from the shoulders to the skull. The trapezius muscle is that muscle in the back of the neck that flares out toward the shoulders. In most weightlifters, bodybuilders, and wrestlers, you will see it as a large, prominent lump on both sides of the base of the neck.

Head Side to Side

The main muscles in the back of the neck are the trapezius muscles. The scalenus muscles (the anterior medius and the posterior scalenus) are muscles on the side of the neck that assist in side to side movement of the head. The trapezius muscle runs from the base of the skull, attaching along the ligamentum nuchae, a strong ligament that runs down the back of the neck, with attachments on the spinous processes of the vertebrae from the seventh cervicle vertebra to the twelfth thoracic vertebra. Although the main exercises for the trapezius muscles are not neck exercises, these muscles benefit from the Head Side to Side exercise mainly through the action of lifting your shoulders as you push your head from side to side. This movement will be utilized as a combination exercise described later. The scalenus muscles will derive the greatest benefit from this neck exercise.

The scalenus muscles will derive the greatest benefit from this neck exercise.

In this exercise the head is pushed in a sideways direction toward one shoulder, using arm and shoulder strength while resisting with the neck muscles (negative phase). The head is then forced back to the opposite shoulder, contracting the neck muscles (positive phase) while the arm and shoulder yield.

Position the palm just above the temple and after performing six repetitions (full shoulder to shoulder head movements), switch to the other arm to work both sides of the neck. The movements should take a count of four in the negative phase and the same time for the positive phase. Remember to maintain constant tension throughout the repetitions. Imagine your life force, "chi," flowing into the muscle with each Yin and Yang movement. This process is important to Autotonics and is utilized for all the following exercises.

HEAD SIDE TO SIDE

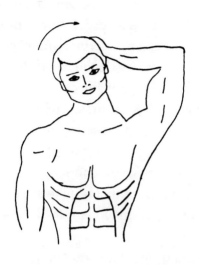

Head Pull

The main head and neck extensors (the muscles involved in lifting the head and moving it backwards) are the spinalis capitis and the semispinalis capitis, the spinalis cervicis and semispinalis cervicis, and the splenus capitis and splenus cervicis muscles. To work the head and neck extensor muscles, we do the Head Pull exercise. Clasp your hands together in back of your head, pull your chin toward your chest, then, resisting with your arms, pull your head back as far as you can. From this position, resisting with your neck, pull your head toward your chest again. Six repetitions with maximum effort will be enough, and will constitute one set.

If you are involved in sports that require strong neck muscles, such as wrestling or boxing, you may want to do additional sets of each neck exercise.

If you have a strong neck, this movement, when modified, can also be used for a combination movement to exercise the lats, as will describe later.

HEAD PULL

Head Push

The third movement for the neck, called the Head Push, involves the anterior muscles of the neck (muscles in the front of the neck), the sternomastoid, longus capitis, and longus cervicis muscles. They are involved in flexation of the head, (the act of bringing your head forward and downward).

Make a fist with each hand, then place your fists together, thumbs touching, and place both fists in this position against your forehead. Bend your neck all the way back—this is your starting position. Now bring your head forward and down, as far as possible, resisting with your arms. A slow, steady pace (about four seconds to complete each movement) is about right. Keep the tension steady, and when your head is all the way forward, push back with your arms and fists, resisting with your neck muscles, until you have reached the starting position again. This completes one repetition. Six repetitions of this movement should be enough.

HEAD PUSH

Chapter Ten

Shoulders

Wide, upright, square shoulders give you a feeling of confidence and an aura of dignity. The man or woman most likely to succeed in business or society is the one with an air of confidence. In addition to the psychological aspect, the physical importance is unending, as we use our shoulder muscles constantly in work and play, especially in sports. There is hardly an athletic activity that doesn't involve shoulder strength: baseball, football, tennis, boxing, and weightlifting, to name but a few. These activities, as well as our daily jobs, benefit by added muscular fitness of the shoulders.

The shoulder is a ball and socket joint that is free to move in almost any plane. The shoulder movements are mediated by a multitude of shoulder, chest, back, and upper arm muscles.

The main shoulder muscle is the deltoid, or "delt." It consists of three separate heads (the anterior, medial or lateral, and the posterior heads), involved in specific functions. The delts are the muscles that cap the shoulders and give them their appearance of thickness and width. Assisting the delts and included in the shoulder muscles is the rotater cuff group, including the subscapularis, infraspinatus, supraspinatus, and teres minor. We will also include in the shoulder group the teres major.

Front Shoulder Raise
This exercise works the anterior head of the deltoid. The anterior deltoid raises the arm in a forward plane to a position in front of your body. It also acts with the pectoralis or chest muscle to bring your arm toward the center of the body, flexing the shoulder. The Front Shoulder Raise utilized the first anatomical function of raising the arm. The second anterior deltoid exercise, the High Pec Push, utilizes the second anatomical function of flexing the shoulder. The anterior head

49

of the deltoid is worked very strongly in the Front Shoulder Raise because of the leverage and the strength of the resisting muscle group.

To perform this exercise you begin with your left arm at your left side, palm facing backwards, and place your right hand over your left hand. Slowly raise the left arm, resisting with the right arm, keeping the left elbow locked, to a position as straight up as possible. Reverse the movement at the top position and pull the left arm down to the starting point. This is one repetition (rep); try for six repetitions. This is an extremely hard exercise, and by six reps your shoulders should experience a burning sensation. This burn is caused by the release of fatigue toxins and signals that the exercise has reached the intensity needed for growth, and has given rise to the cliche "no pain, no gain." Believe me, this is one movement in which you will certainly experience pain. This particular exercise is an excellent one in which to employ another bodybuilding technique, "training past failure." Usually, by the time you have done six repetitions, you won't be able to raise your arm anymore, but will still be able to resist pulling your arm down from the top end position. These kinds of movements are referred to as "negatives." Once you have reached positive failure, the inability to raise your arms, you still possess strength in resisting, lowering of the arms, or negative resistance. This can be employed to further fatigue the muscle and make faster gains in muscle growth, but should probably be used only every third workout to keep from overtraining, and should be utilized only after several months of training.

FRONT SHOULDER RAISE

High Pec Push

This is actually a combination exercise and will be utilized as such in the workout routines to be given later. This exercise works both the anterior deltoid and the pectoralis major muscle. This exercise should also be used to build muscle in the upper portion of the chest as it blends in with the shoulder, giving a more esthetic appearance or flow from shoulder to chest.

Place your hands together over and in front of your head, as if you were clapping in a crowd. Bring your left arm to your left cheek, resisting hard with your right shoulder; then push back with your right arm and shoulder until your right arm touches your right cheek. This is considered a repetition. Maintain the tension and repeat the pushing movements back and forth for twelve half repetitions (each touch is one half rep) or six full repetitions with each arm. This constitutes one set.

Avoid turning your cheek to meet your arm. Try to keep your head stationary, facing forward, and make your shoulders contract to their full extent. This movement is slow and concentrated, as are all Autotonic movements; a count of four for each half rep is about right.

HIGH PEC PUSH

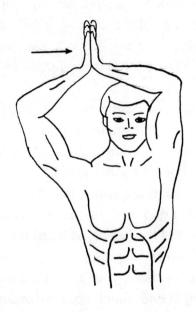

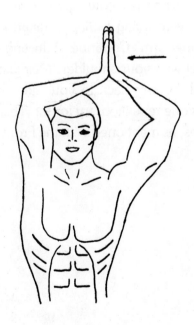

53

Lateral Shoulder Raise

The lateral or medial head of the deltoid and the supraspinatus muscle that lies underneath it are the main muscles of abduction of the shoulder and arm. Abduction is the action it takes to move the arms away from the body if they are in a vertical plane or hanging at your sides.

To work the lateral deltoid head, resistance must be applied as the arm abducts. In bodybuilding, the exercise performed to work this muscle is called the lateral raise with dumbbells. With Autotonics we also perform a lateral raise, but with some modifications. Instead of keeping the arm straight, we bend the arm at the elbow. This serves two purposes: it allows a better grip on the arm and also reduces any assistance from the long head of the biceps, so it creates an isolation movement for the lateral deltoid and supraspinatus.

With your arms at your sides, bend your arm at the elbow ninety degrees with the palm facing in and thumb up; now make a fist with your hand. Reach across your body with your opposite hand and grasp your wrist. Keeping the elbow rigid, move your arm away from the body as if you were trying to flap your arm like a wing. Resist strongly with the other arm. Continue abducting until it is at a slight angle above parallel with your shoulder. Maintain the tension at the high point and pull the arm back to your side, staying in the same arc. This completes one repetition; try for six. This exercise also lends itself to negative reps, as mentioned with the Front Shoulder Raise.

LATERAL SHOULDER RAISE

Lateral Shoulder Pull

Another movement that works the medial section of the deltoid, and the posterior and upper trapezius muscles as well, can be used as an alternative exercise or in combination with the lateral raise to bring the medial deltoids to complete failure, called a compound movement. This is a training method highly touted by Mike Mentzer, a champion bodybuilder and creator of the Heavy Duty Training System. According to the Heavy Duty Training System, the first set of an exercise used is called an isolation movement, one that concentrates on the particular muscle, and that exercise is carried to positive failure. Positive failure is a point where the contractile phase can no longer be completed, such as raising the arm in the Lateral Shoulder Raise. Then you go immediately to another exercise that is considered a compound movement (one in which other muscles assist in the movement). In doing so, the target muscle, such as the medial deltoid already exhausted by the lateral raise, can be worked even more intensely because it will be assisted by other muscles. To get a muscle to grow at its fastest rate, you have to work it with extreme intensity, but with caution not to overdo, because over-training will result and injury can occur. If you are going to try this type of training, two sets are about all your muscles can endure.

To do the compound movement that I call Lateral Shoulder Pull, grasp your hands at solar plexus level, cupping the fingers of one hand into the fingers of the other, one palm facing up and the other down. Now pull sideways in an arc, moving your elbow up and to the side. You carry the movement until the shoulder starts to rise above a line paralled with the opposite shoulder. If you continue any further, and the shoulder starts to lift, the upper trapezius muscle will come into play. You may want to add this upper movement in the trapezius workout, or use it as a combination exercise. Remember to switch hand positions at six reps, doing twelve total half reps, or six full reps, for each shoulder. This constitutes one set.

LATERAL SHOULDER PULL

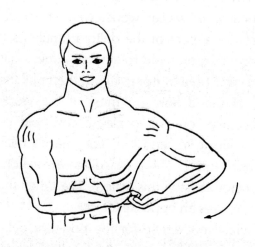

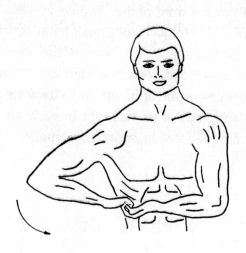

Posterior Deltoid Pull - P.D. Pull

The posterior deltoid exercises bring into action many other helper muscles; therefore, it is difficult to isolate the posterior deltoid like the other two heads, but we can work it very hard nevertheless.

The posterior aspect of the deltoid functions to extend the arm from a horizontal plane and rotate the humerus laterally. If you hold your arms straight out in front of you, then pull them backwards, the rear fibers of the deltoid do most of the work. Rotation of the humerus laterally comes into play if you hold your hands at your sides, palms facing in, and turn your hands palms facing out until the upper arms rotate. This is called lateral rotation. The infraspinatus and teres minor assist in this action. The other shoulder muscle, the teres major, causes an opposite effect.

A very effective exercise for the posterior deltoid I call the P.D. Pull. Clasp your hands as you did for the Lateral Pull, cupping the fingers together in front of your chest and six inches away from it, the back of one hand toward the chest and the palm of the other hand toward the chest, fingers cupped. Pull with one arm while resisting with the other. Try to pull far enough to touch the knuckles of the opposite hands to the front of the shoulder, pulling back and forth slowly and strongly. Each touch constitutes a half repetition. Try for twelve half reps. Be cautious at first, because this exercise puts a heavy strain on the shoulder joint. You may want to vary the distance from your chest and move your arms up and down for variations in the pull. Also switch hands at six half reps in each set. Maintain continuous tension with slow, steady, strong movements.

POSTERIOR DELTOID PULL- P.D. PULL

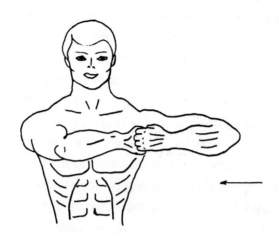

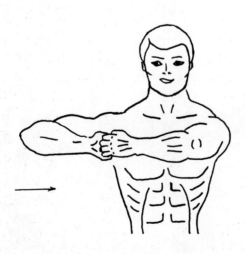

Lateral Shoulder Rotation

By rotating (twisting) the upper arm laterally or away from the body, you work the teres minor and infraspinatus muscles along with the posterior deltoid muscle. Begin with the arm bent in the same manner as described with the Lateral Shoulder Raise. Grasping the bent arm in the same manner at the wrist, pull the bent arm against your stomach. This will be your starting position. From this position, swing the forearm out sideways, keeping your elbow tucked in. Swing it out, resisting with the opposite arm, as far to the side as possible. When you have reached the farthest position, keep the tension and pull the arm back toward the stomach or starting position. From starting position to starting position is one rep. Try for six slow, concentrated reps. You will feel muscles working that you probably never felt before, because this exercise really isolates the infraspinatus and teres minor muscles.

LATERAL SHOULDER ROTATION

Medial Shoulder Rotation

This exercise utilizes the same arm position as the previous exercise, the Lateral Shoulder Rotation, but because the arm is resisted against its medial rotation, it works different muscle groups. In this exercise the teres major and pectoralis major muscles are worked. The teres major lies below the teres minor and above the latissimus dorsi muscle. If you want to get an idea of their anatomic positions, watch in the mirror as you go through the movements, and you should see your target muscle contracting.

To do this exercise begin with the same arm positions as described for the Lateral Shoulder Rotation, except that the starting position will be with the arm swung out to the side. Starting there, pull the forearm toward the abdomen and push it back again to the start. This is one rep. Try for six reps. Count to four pulling in and four pushing out. Don't let up on the tension at any point.

MEDIAL SHOULDER ROTATION

Arms

The arms are probably the part of the anatomy most displayed to signify power and strength. They have been utilized again and again in commercials to sell the idea of strength. Their aesthetic appeal aside, they are certainly handy levers indeed. Their utilizations in sports and daily life are so numerous and so necessary that they are without need of examination. To seek out means to increase their maximum size, strength, and definition should concern all health enthusiasts, no matter what their goal or sport.

At the end of the arm is the fantastic instrument called the hand, with its opposing thumb that sets us apart in the animal world. The hand contains many muscles of its own but is controlled by muscles of the forearm. The wrist is capable of movements in many planes and is controlled by muscles of the forearm, also. The forearm contains the muscles that control the hand and wrist, and also a few muscles that flex the elbow and twist the forearm. The upper arm contains the muscles that bend and extend the elbow and are involved to a slight degree with shoulder movement.

The upper flexors are the biceps brachii and brachialis muscles. The brachialis is a pure elbow flexor, but the biceps also supinates the hand and helps with shoulder flexion in addition to flexing the elbow.

The upper arm extensor is the triceps brachii muscle. This muscle is divided into three separate heads that join in a strong tendon which attaches to the elbow bone (the olecranon process of the ulna) and acts primarily to extend the elbow. Because of its attachments to the scapula, it also assists in some shoulder movements.

Biceps Curl

The biceps brachii, the large muscle of the upper arm, is the first one flexed as a show of strength. It consists of two heads, the long and the short head. Both heads attach to the scapula at different places and span the shoulder joint. They join together in a strong tendon that attaches to the radius bone of the forearm. The biceps muscle spans both joints. Its first function is to supinate the hand (turn the palm upward). Its second function is to flex the elbow, and it is involved in assisting the flexion of the shoulder.

We will explore all three functions of this muscle in the following exercises.

The classic biceps exercise is the curl, and Autotonics fulfills the requirements of this exercise very nicely. In a standing position, beginning with one arm extended at your side, make a partial fist in a supinated position (palm facing upward). Cup your opposite hand over the wrist, overlapping the palm. Keeping the elbow tucked into your side, bring your forearm toward your shoulder in an arc, resisting with the opposite arm. Continue to supinate your hand and contract your arm at the same time as far as you can go. Now reverse the motion back to the starting position, pushing your arm back down while resisting all the way with the biceps muscle. Six full repetitions from starting point to starting point, if done slowly and with one hundred percent effort, should bring you to positive failure with a nice "pump" in the biceps. In bodybuilding lingo a "pump" refers to the swelling sensation of a muscle as a large amount of blood is trapped within the capillaries (small blood vessels feeding the muscle). The pump is another condition strived for by bodybuilders, as it signals that the muscle is getting a good workout. This exercise can be carried on to negative failure or utilized with burns or forced reps, which I will discuss later.

BICEPS CURL

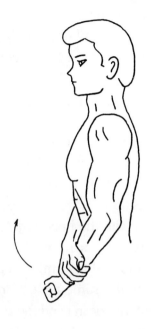

Special Autotonics Curl

The Biceps Curl utilizes two of the anatomic functions of the biceps muscle, supination and flexion, but the Special Autotonics Curl allows you to perform a movement that incorporates all three functions of the bicep: supination of the hand, flexion of the elbow joint, and flexion of the shoulder joint.

This is a legitimate exercise, and worth trying to learn, but because it involves many different movements, it is complicated, difficult, and requires some practice. It is a movement that would be hard for machine to duplicate, but because your body is such an ingenious machine, it allows these complicated functions.

Assume the regular curl position, except that you grip your wrist a little farther up. Begin the curl with the hand slightly pronated (palm facing back) and try to supinate the arm, resisting with the gripping hand; at the same time begin to curl the arm. Keep the pressure on the arm to supinate the curl at the same time. Bring the arm to full flexion. However, the movement doesn't end there. Keeping the arm in flexion and maintaining supination tension, bring your arm up flexing the shoulder, and continue pulling it back as if you were trying to punch someone standing behind you. This movement also flexes the biceps at the upper end because of its attachments to the scapula. Bring the arm back down again, continuing the supination tension and negative contraction of the biceps. This is the ultimate curl. Try it, you might like it. If you do it right, you should feel a very strong contraction in the biceps muscle, which will start to burn after six reps. Try at least six slow, concentrated, strong contractions.

SPECIAL AUTOTONICS CURL

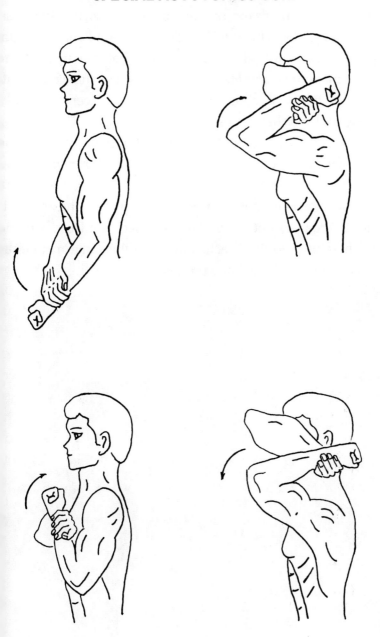

Brachialis Curl

The other important flexor of the upper arm is the brachialis muscle, which attaches to the humerus at its lower end and lies under the biceps. It crosses the elbow and attaches to the ulna of the forearm. The main function of the brachialis is to flex the elbow joint and in this function it is about as strong as the biceps. It works about equally well in all hand positions.

Since the biceps works best in the supinated position, you can use this to advantage by working the brachialis in the pronated hand position (palm facing down).

Because the biceps tendon is twisted, the pull on the biceps is nullified to a great extent, and the workload is placed on the brachialis. Therefore, do the Brachialis Curl in the same manner as the Biceps Curl, only with the hand pronated.

BRACHIALIS CURL

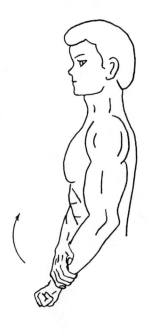

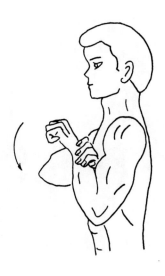

Brachioradialis Curl

Using the curl movement with the hand in the neutral position brings the brachioadialis muscle more into action. The brachioradialis is a muscle of the forearm, but it crosses the elbow joint and helps to flex the arm. The biceps and brachialis work about equally from this position, as well as the brachioradialis, so the neutral position works all three flexors. Using all three positions as a tri-set or super-set will really give the flexors a workout. A tri-set or super-set is a continuous set using each one of the three curl variations for six reps with no rest in between. This is yet another bodybuilding technique used to build muscle faster. All of these special techniques will be discussed again in a later chapter.

BRACHIORADIALIS CURL

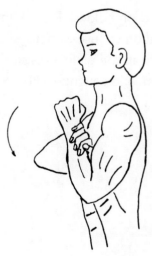

Seated Curl

I would like to introduce one more curling movement for two reasons. First, it works the biceps from a different angle and second it enables you to work both biceps at the same time, thus saving time and providing variety. I find this curl to work best while sitting on the floor, legs stretched out in front. Keeping your back straight reach forward and grasp your leg behind the knee. From this position put your knee toward your chin resisting with your leg. This will bring the arms out to the side in a wing like fashion. Concentrate on flexing the biceps as far as possible by trying to touch your knee to the chin if you can. Return your leg to the floor by reversing the movement and resistance. If you plan one set of six reps change legs at three reps to insure equal and similar tension on both arms. If you are doing more than one set switch legs with each set.

Some mistakes in form that you should try to avoid are; bending over to far toward the leg as this will limit the range of arm contraction, and put too much strain on the back; pulling the leg into the chest, as this will activate the latissimus dorsi muscles reducing tension on the biceps.

Keep the movement smooth and slow. Try for three curls with each leg. This exercise is a good one to use with negative contraction because of the superior strength in the gluteal resistor muscles it will be easy to achieve positive failure and continue with negatives.

SEATED CURL

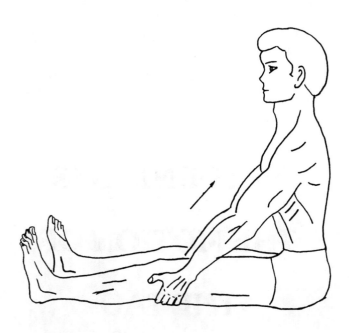

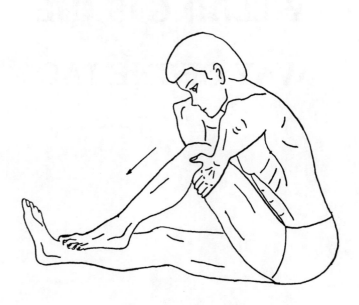

RETURNING IS THE MOTION OF THE TAO YIELDING IS THE WAY OF THE TAO

FROM: TAO TE CHING

Long Head Triceps Extension

The extender of the elbow is the triceps muscle, the muscle that contributes most to the bulk of the upper arm. Do not neglect this in your workouts.

The triceps, as the name implies, has three sections, the lateral, medial, and long heads. The long head, which attaches to the scapula and crosses the shoulder joint, contributes to adducting the arm as well as extending the elbow. The lateral and medial heads arise from the shaft of the humerus and converge into a single tendon that attaches to the olecranon process of the ulna or point of the elbow.

All three heads contribute to extension of the elbow, but placing the arm and hand in different positions places more stress on different heads and contributes to fastest maximum growth of the muscle, as well as muscle shaping.

The long head is best worked with the arm in a vertical upright position.

Reach straight up with the arm and make a fist, then grasp the fist with the opposite hand, palm to fist. As you pull the extended arm and hand down toward the back of the neck, bending the arm at the elbow, resisting with the triceps, you should feel quite a bit of tension in the long head of the triceps. Pull down and try to flex the arm to the full extent. Keep constant tension even in the flexed position and then extend the arm back to the starting position. Slow and steady, about four seconds down and four seconds to return, constitutes a rep. Six reps should have your arm burning with fatique toxins. If you wish to push past positive failure, continue with negative reps. When you arm is too tired to extend itself against resistance, return to the extended position without resistance, and then pull your arm back to the flexed position until you have no further strength in this negative phase, or negative failure.

LONG HEAD TRICEPS EXTENSION

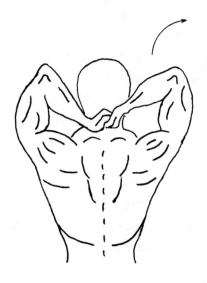

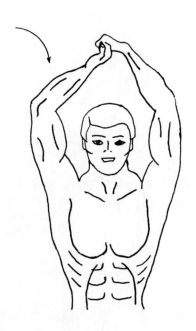

Medial Head Triceps Extension

The medial head of the triceps is located at the back of the upper arm closest to the body when the arm is in a hanging position. In the curl, you worked the biceps muscle by resisting flexion or bending of the elbow. The Medial Head Triceps Extension is a reverse of this movement: you try to extend or straighten the elbow while resisting with the opposite arm. Begin this movement with the arm in the position you had in the curl movement, with the elbow fully bent. Make the hand into a fist with the palm facing down. From this position try to straighten your arm (extend your elbow) while resisting with the other arm. When the arm is fully extended, pull the arm back to the starting position, resisting with the triceps muscle. This is one rep. Try for six reps with each arm.

MEDIAL HEAD TRICEPS EXTENSION

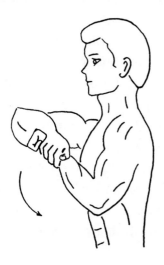

Lateral Head Triceps Extension

The lateral head of the triceps is located on the back of the upper arm on the side away from the body when the arm is hanging at the side. When developed fully, this portion assumes a horseshoe shape. The exercise for this portion is done in the same manner as for the Medial Head except that the palm is facing up. Six reps with both arms constitutes a set. Using all three of these movements in a row, or super-setting them, will really pump your triceps. Working them to negative failure on each movement with rests in between will do the same. These types of movements should be used only by more advanced bodybuilders. Beginners, or those interested only in good all-around body conditioning, should begin with one set of any of the three movements, reserving the others for the next workout to provide variety.

LATERAL HEAD TRICEPS EXTENSION

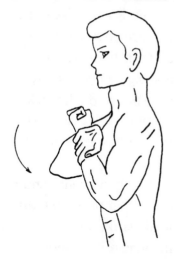

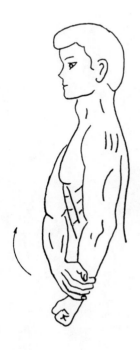

Triceps Bent Press

To perform the Triceps Bent Press, place the legs together, bending the knees slightly and place your hands on your knees. With the hands on the knees, pull your body into a squatting position, resisting with the arms. Then straighten your body again by pushing with the arms. In this position the triceps do the bulk of the work. The movement is continued for a count of six reps. The legs and trunk are used as the resistor muscles in this exercise; therefore, you can really work the triceps hard.

You may want to experiment with different hand positions on this one, also. Knuckles toward each other puts more stress on the lateral head. Knuckles straight ahead works the long head more, and knuckles turned out stresses the medial head more.

TRICEPS BENT PRESS

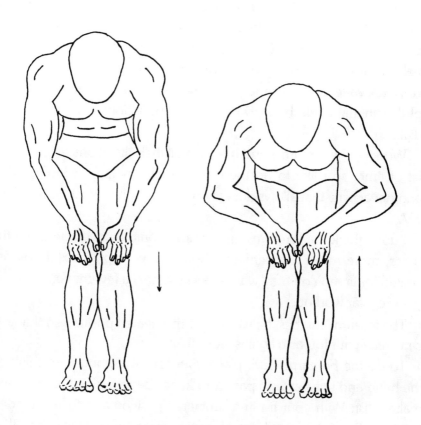

Forearm Curl

I've always been impressed by big forearms. They seem to complete that picture of potential strength in the arm. Besides the look, they provide that grip strength that you feel in a firm handshake and that you use to get a good grip on your tennis racket, your golf clubs, baseball bat etc. or anything else that requires a good strong grip.

The muscles in the forearms extend and flex your fingers and thumbs through their tendons. They flex and extend the wrist and to some degree rotate it. They pronate and supinate the forearms and help to flex the elbow. There are twenty muscles that provide this complex variety of movements and set us humans apart from the rest of the animal world by allowing us the opposition of the thumb and digits.

Working the forearms and hands in all their directions takes quite a bit of time, so I like to do these movements when I'm occupied in another activity that allows doing two things at once, such as watching TV.

I don't think the forearms and hands should be neglected, but the other, more major, movements should be your priorities if you are limited for time. You may want to include only a few movements into your regular workout.

The forearm can best be worked from a seated position so that you can brace your forearm against your thigh.

To do the Forearm Curl, place your forearm along your thigh so the hand and wrist extend past your knee. Begin with either arm and make a fist. With your fist in a supinated position and fully extended (back of fist against the front of knee), grasp the fist with the other hand and curl the fist and wrist up into a fully flexed position, resisting with your other arm. Now push it back, resisting all the time, into the extended position again. These are short movements, but again remember to concentrate and go through the movements slowly, resisting hard, and you will really get a good workout.

FOREARM CURL

Forearm Extension

Keeping the arm and fist in the same position as the Forearm Curl, you work the extensor muscles of the forearm by resisting the extension action of the wrist. Beginning with the wrist in a curled position, grasp it with the opposite hand. Bend the fist down (extend it) until it touches the knee, then pull it back while resisting, thus reversing the movements of the previous exercise. Do six slow, concentrated reps of this exercise with each arm.

FOREARM EXTENSION

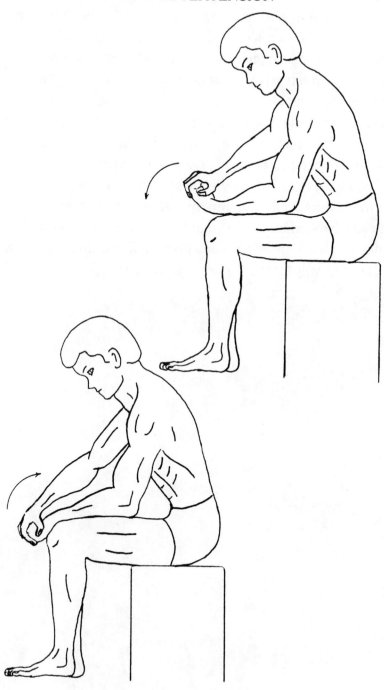

Forearm Twist

The forearms also pronate and supinate the hand, and this function can be worked with a twisting exercise. Cup the hands together with the fingers, then alternately rotate the forearms, first one way then the other, resisting both ways. Change hand position after six reps and perform another six reps with the different hand position. This can still be accomplished from the sitting position, resting the elbows on the thighs. Twelve repetitions, switching positions at six reps, should conclude your forearm workout.

If you want to include any of these with your regular workout, you can rotate through the different movements and again add variety to your regular workout. If you want a concentrated forearm workout, fit this in your regular workout twice a week, and you should be well on your way for the next Popeye screen test.

FOREARM TWIST

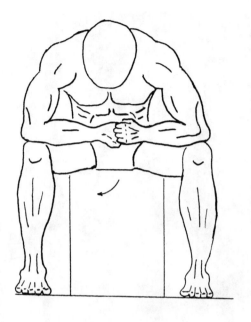

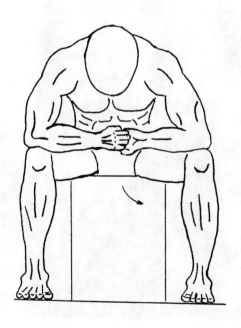

Chapter Eleven

Chest

"Suck in that stomach! Stick out that chest! Show some pride in yourself!" This military cliche exemplifies the idea that a swelled chest conveys pride in your appearance and usually signifies pride in your work and pride in yourself. Pride doesn't mean arrogance, which is a forced look. A well-built chest naturally stands out, and the appearance is recognized without strain.

This body part, commonly referred to by iron pumpers as "pecs," is composed of the pectoralis major and pectoralis minor muscles. These two separate muscles of the chest have different origins and attachments, and these anatomical differences can be used, as we have seen in previous muscle groups, to work each muscle fully.

The pectoralis major originates from the sternum, the first six ribs, and abdominal muscles and inserts on the humerus or upper arm. Its action is to flex the shoulder, rotate the arm medially, adduct the arm, and depress the shoulder girdle (pull the clavicle and scapula downward).

The pectoralis minor arises from the third, fourth, and fifth ribs and attaches to the coracoid process of the scapula. Its major function is to pull the shoulder forward.

Another minor muscle that assists in adducting the arm and flexing the shoulder is the coracobrachialis. It adds nothing to the mass of the chest, and is mentioned only in passing.

The serratus anterior muscle, which assists in pulling the scapula forward and rotating it outwardly, will be worked along with the pectoralis major and minor muscles. The serratus muscles are seen (if you are lean) as lumps that resemble ribs starting under your arm pit and along the side of your body. Where the serratus muscles end, the intercostals begin (the muscles between the ribs,) blending into the waist with the external abdominal obliques. If a bodybuilder is really "ripped" (bodybuilder lingo for lean) and developed, and displays his or her side in the classic bodybuilder pose, you will see a continuous series of lumpy muscles rippling down the side from the armpit to the hip. With Autotonics you can work toward significant improvement of the chest group from several different angles.

High Pec Push

This pec exercise was mentioned earlier, with the shoulder movements. The anterior deltoid assists in the movement and helps to tie in the upper pecs with the shoulder.

Place your hands together over your head as if you were clapping. Start by moving your arms to the right so that your left bicep touches your left cheek (you can begin with either arm). Move the right hand toward the right cheek, resisting with the left. Try to keep your face straight ahead and avoid reaching your cheek toward your arm. Make yourself push the arms through their full range of motion. Move back and forth with constant tension for a count of twelve cheek touches. The movement is short, so you must concentrate and resist hard enough to get a count of four between touches.

Pec Push

This second exercise will bring into play the greater mass of the pectoralis major along with the pectoralis minor and serratus anterior muscle. This exercise utilized two of the five anatomical functions of the chest; shoulder flexion and pulling the shoulders forward.

Bring the hands together in front of the chest, as if clapping or praying (you may want to think of this as praying for a bigger, thicker chest or as applauding yourself for the progress you have already made). The hands will be out in front of your chest approximately six inches. By moving the hands closer or farther away, you can vary the angle and intensity, but you also shorten the range of movement. You should use the six inch distance for your basic movement and then vary the movement as it suits you.

In this exercise I like to touch my thumbs to my shoulders as I move my arms back and forth in front of my chest. Start with either side, move the arms back and forth, resisting as hard as you can, touching the thumbs to the shoulder for each rep. Twelve reps, slow and concentrated, will work the pectoralis major by flexing the shoulder and will work the pectoralis minor and serratus anterior by bringing the shoulder forward at the end of the movement.

PEC PUSH

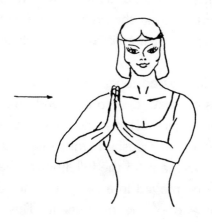

Low Pec Push

Using another arm position, the lower portion of the pectoral muscle can be exercised. This movement employs the adduction of the arm while flexing the shoulder and medial rotating the arms. Also, because of the arm position, the shoulder girdle is depressed (pulled downward), thus using the pectoralis major muscle in all four of its anatomical functions.

The hands are again pressed together in the clapping or praying position, but the arms are extended so the hands are in front of the lower abdomen. The object of this movement is similar to the previous two. The hands are pushed from one side to the other in a slow, pendular movement, to the full limits of their side to side movement. They can be moved in a straight plane, or pulled in to touch the hip at the end of the movement. This will bring the shoulder forward, working the pectoralis minor and serratus muscles.

These three movements, the Pec Push, the High Pec Push, and the Low Pec Push, are a natural for a tri-set or a super-set, to work the upper, middle, and lower portions of the pecs as well as all their anatomic functions. Twelve reps should be your target.

LOW PEC PUSH

Pec Squeeze

Using dumbbells, a common exercise for chest development is the "fly." You lie on your back, on a bench, a dumbbell in each hand hands out from your chest to the side with the elbows slightly bent. The dumbells are brought up in an arc, over the chest thus flexing the shoulders. The Nautilus machine has its own variation of that movement. In a seated position, you place your elbows against pads attached to the machine and rotate your upper arm in an arc from a position at your sides to a position in front of your chest. This movement flexes the shoulders and works the chest.

Autotonics has its own version of the fly movement, the Pec Squeeze. This movement, in a slightly different version, can also be used to work the abductor muscles of the legs and hips.

Sit on the floor with your knees bent. Place your wrists on the outside of your knees and spread your legs, resisting with the pec muscles. Bring your arms together, contracting your pec muscles until the knees touch each other, then spread your knees again. One set, consists of six reps, knee spread to knee spread, and if you are applying maximum effort, that will probably be all that you can do. Of course, you continue with negatives, if you want more of a workout. After you have exhausted the ability to squeeze your knees together with your arms, bring your knees together and push your arms apart in the negative phase.

PEC SQUEEZE

Bent Press Wide Stance and Medium Stance

This chest exercise resembles the Farnham Standing Crunch, a abdominal exercise, but it utilizes different body movements tha strongly emphasize the pectoralis muscles. It is similar in executio to the bench press, a common bodybuilding movement, and becaus of the similarity, I have named it the Bent Press.

Bend at the waist and place your hands on your knees. From th position, perform a compound movement of squatting and bendin at the waist, resisting with your arms and chest. Pull yourself towar your knees. Your legs should be placed far enough apart at the sta so that your torso can end up between your knees. Try to bend an squat low enough so that your chest is almost parallel with the tops o your thighs and your arms are bent strongly, elbows out. From th position push up again to arms length, resisting with the torso. Tr six reps of this Bent Press and feel the similarity to the bench press This movement can also be continued with negative reps if you desire.

By changing the width of your stance from wide to narrow you ca emphasize different muscles. With a very wide stance the pecs wor harder; a normal stance brings the anterior deltoids and triceps mor into play; and the narrow stance, knees together, works the tricep primarily.

BENT PRESS WIDE STANCE AND MEDIUM STANCE

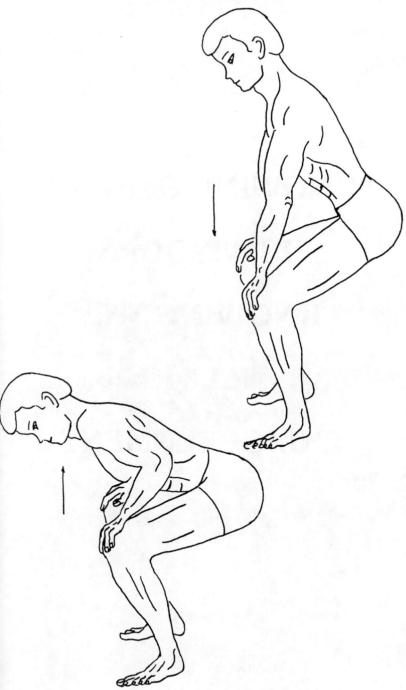

KNOWING OTHERS

IS WISDOM

KNOWING THE

SELF IS

ENLIGHTENMENT

FROM: TAO TE CHING

Chapter Twelve

Back - Upper

The number of people with back problems is a shame. Poo posture, lost work time, decreased activity and enjoyment of life pain, despair, and suffering—the very thought of these should make anyone want to strengthen his back so as to avoid these pitfalls.

In a car accident about six years ago I suffered a compressio fracture of my eleventh thoracic vertebra, among other injurie: Because I was left with a protruding area of my spine, I tend to ben slightly and must constantly make a conscious effort to keep straigh I looked at myself in the mirror a few weeks after the accident, and more pathetic sight I wouldn't want to see. Black and blue an swollen, I stood with my shoulders stooped forward, bent over like a eighty-year-old man. I vowed that I would never let this turn me int an invalid or a whiner. A couple of months ago, at the age o forty-three, and weighing 145 pounds, I deadlifted (lifted a barbe from the floor to above my knees) 450 pounds. My goal is 50 pounds—and beyond. Although this isn't a prodigious lift for mo powerlifters, it proves a point. We can all do something abou strengthening our backs and keeping our vitality and health.

Different exercises emphasize specific muscles of the back. There fore, to understand these actions better, let's divide the back int three areas: upper, middle, and lower. We shall focus in this sectio on the upper back.

Several muscles of the upper back that have been mentione previously in connection with the shoulder exercises are the trapeziu: rhomboideus, infraspinatus, supraspinatus, teres major, and tere minor. I arbitrarily grouped then with the shoulder exercises becaus of their involvement with shoulder movements. They can also b considered upper back muscles because of their anatomic locatior In this chapter on back exercises I will consider the trapezius muscle a

106

he primary upper back muscle. The trapezius attaches from the base of the skull down to the last thoracic vertebra and to the scapula and the clavicle. It lifts the shoulders and brings them together. This action s assisted by the rhomboid muscles that also adduct the scapula. The evator scapula lying under the trapezius also assists in lifting the houlder via the scapula or shoulder blade.

The infraspinatus and teres minor muscle along the lower portion f the scapula connect the scapula and arm and rotate the arm aterally.

The exercises best suited for the development of some of the upper ack muscles were discussed in connection with the shoulders, ncluding the medial and lateral shoulder rotation and the Posterior Deltoid Pull or P.D. Pull, which bring into action the posterior deltoid, apezius, and rhomboid muscles. The medial shoulder rotation xercises the teres major. The lateral shoulder rotation exercises the nfraspinatus and teres minor muscle. The Head Side to Side and the ateral Pull carried higher than the parallel shoulder position will ork the trapezius muscle.

Now let's move on to several more exercises that will work the apezius with much greater intensity, beginning with the High Trap ull.

ligh Trap Pull

Earlier, I called this movement the Lateral Shoulder Pull and used to work the medial and posterior deltoid sections. The hands were rasped in the finger cup grip and the arms pulled back and forth ntil the upper arms were at the point where they started to lift the houlder above parallel.

For the High Trap Pull variation, starting at slightly below the arallel point, continue the movement, trying to squeeze your houlder to your ear; even though the arc is short, try to move in a low, concentrated manner. Try to feel the trapezius lifting the houlder and pulling it toward your neck. The "bunching up" feeling

you will get at the back of your neck between your neck and shoulde
is the upper portion of the trapezius. Make this muscle work by feelin
it. Six to eight reps should work the muscle well.

HIGH TRAP PULL

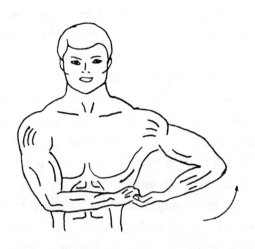

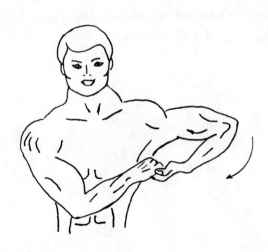

Standing Shoulder Shrug

One of the standard exercises used by bodybuilders for the upper traps is called the shoulder shrug. This movement, as well as other bodybuilding movements for the traps, involves lifting the shoulder against resistance. The Autotonics Shoulder Shrug utilizes the same principle, but the means of resistance is quite different. Weight trainers use dumbbells and barbells for resistance. The Nautilus Company has also designed a machine to provide this kind of resistance. Autotonics uses the leg muscles as the resistor.

This exercise requires that you stand on one leg, so it is a good idea to use a chair or wall to balance yourself. Grasp one leg below the knee, keeping your arm straight, and lift that resisting leg as high as possible, using only your trapezius muscle. The arm acts only to connect the leg and shoulder. The trapezius, as stated, lifts the shoulders, so try to bring the shoulder toward your ear (shrug your shoulders). Keep your head straight and feel the trapezius squeeze into a ball at the base of your neck. Pause for a second at the top of the shrug, then pull your shoulders down, using the leg. This is a difficult exercise because it is hard to keep a good grip on the leg, and it is difficult to feel the proper movement, but persevere and you shall overcome. Try for six reps.

STANDING SHOULDER SHRUG

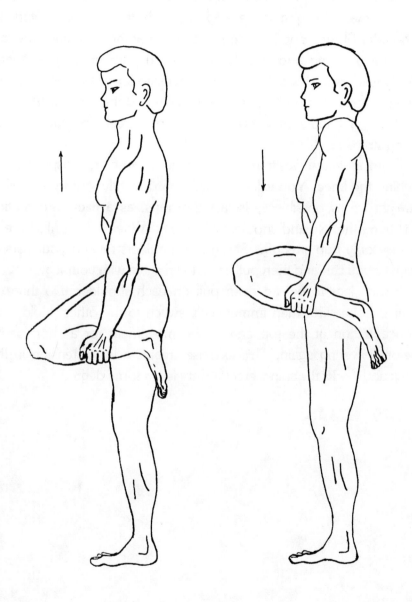

Seated Shoulder Shrug

Another shoulder shrug, which many people will find somewhat easier to perform, is done from a seated position. The problem still lies in maintaining a good grip, as with the one-arm Standing Shoulder Shrug. You have to remember that the trapezius muscle is extremely strong and usually can exceed your gripping strength. Bodybuilders and weight lifters compensate for this by using heavy cotton straps wrapped around the barbells and their wrists. (As small as I am, I handle over 500 pounds for barbell shoulder shrugs, using straps.)

From a seated position on the edge of a chair, grasp your leg behind the knee. You will be bent forward slightly, but try to pull as straight up as possible to isolate the traps, as a backward motion will bring the lats and shoulders into play. When I say pull, I mean to use only trap strength. Shrug the shoulders toward your ears as high as you can and then pull back down again with your leg.

Switch legs to get an even pull on each shoulder. Do three to four on one side, then immediately switch to the other. Hold your concentration at the top end of the movement for a short pause before lowering again. This exercise creates a lot of tension in the back and works the spinal erector muscles to some degree.

SEATED SHOULDER SHRUG

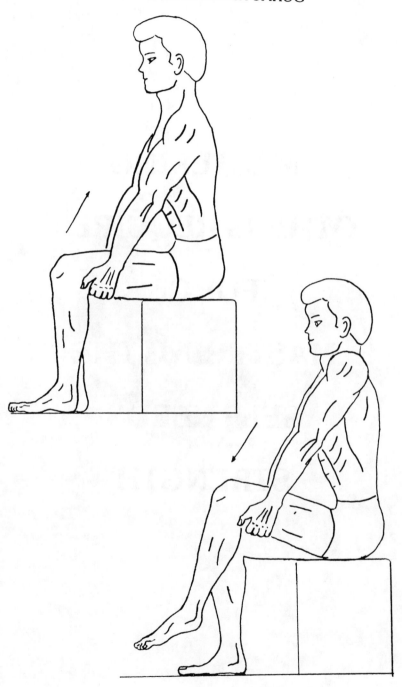

MASTERING

OTHERS REQUIRES

FORCE

MASTERING THE

SELF NEEDS

STRENGTH

FROM: TAO TE CHING

114

Chapter Thirteen

Back - Middle

In the middle portion of the back lies the large latissimus dorsi muscle or the "lats," as they are affectionately called. They start from the waist and spread out under the arms to give that "V-shaped" build. The lats originate from the vertebral spines of the last six thoracic and lumbar vertebra, the strong fibrous tissue of the back called the lumbordorsal fascia, the top of the hip bone called the ilium, some of the lower ribs, and a small portion of the scapula. The fibers blend together and attach to the upper arm bone called the humerus. The lats pull the arms toward the body, or adducts the arms; pulls the arms back, or extends them; and is used very strongly when climbing or pulling the body up.

The main weight exercises that work the lats are called rows, bent-over dumbbell or barbell rows, T-bar rows, and seated row. Also employed are chins, in front of or behind the neck. Another weight training exercise is called pull downs, where the body remains stationary, and lats pull weights, attached via a pulley system, down to the chest or behind the neck.

These movements utilize the anatomical function of pulling the body up or extending the humerus (pulling the arms back). Autotonics utilizes similar rowing movements with body resistance, plus another movement that works the adduction function.

Autotonics utilizes the bent-over row to work the bulk of the muscle and the crossbody row to work the lats from a different angle, as well as really give them a good stretch, which is touted by body-builders as a boon to their development.

Bent Over Row

The Bent Over Row is done very similarly to the one-arm bent-over row with a dumbbell, except that we use the leg for the resistance. Assume a bent over position, supporting yourself with one hand on a bench or chair. With the other hand, grasp the leg below the knee. Now pull the resisting leg toward your chest, as tight as you can, and hold this tension for a count of two, then push the leg down slowly, resisting strongly with the latissimus muscle. Six full reps is about all you can do if using one hundred percent effort. Although the target muscle is the latissimus muscle, many other upper back muscles are involved in this exercise. The biceps muscle also comes into assistance. For this reason this exercise has been utilized as a compound movement in the section describing the exercise routines.

BENT OVER ROW

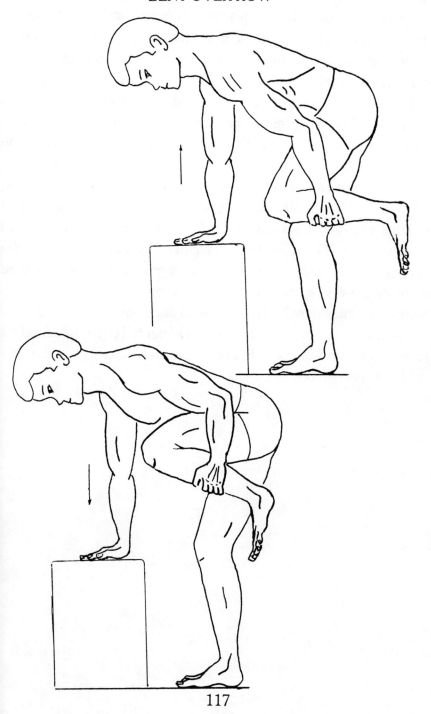

Cross Body Row

The Cross Body Row works the lats from a different angle and stretches them at the end of the movement. This movement is somewhat easier to do than the Bent Over Row, and really stretches the muscle as well.

To perform this movement also, you need a chair or bench to place your foot on. Starting with either side, place one foot on a chair or bench. Grasp your knee with the opposite hand, move the knee outwardly until your arm is stretched out across your body. The other arm can be placed behind your back. From this starting position, pull your body toward your leg in a rowing motion, using your lat muscle, resisting strongly with your hips. Pull yourself as far as you can, then reverse the movement, moving your hips to the starting position while resisting with the lat muscle. Extend your knee as far as possible at the end of the movement and feel the stretch in your latissimus muscle. Try six reps on each side.

Just a footnote to this particular movement. To get an added lat stretch, you can twist your hip backward from your leg as the arm reaches full extension.

CROSS BODY ROW

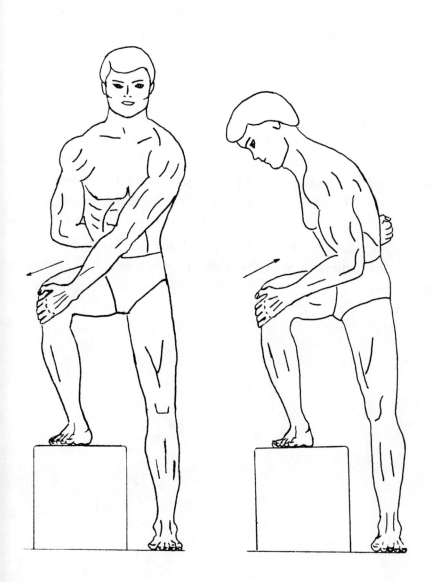

Overhead Lat Pull

The two previous exercises have concentrated on extension of the arm to flex the latissimus. With Autotonics you can utilize the adduction function of the lats. The lat pulldown or chinning movements work the adduction to some degree while working the pulling aspect of muscle.

The Autotonics Overhead Lat Pull works adduction at the top range of the movement. Grasp your hands in the finger cupping grip that has been used previously. Hands behind the head at about head level, begin with either arm, start with the pulling arm abducted fully, the biceps touching the back of the head and arm in a vertical position. If your right arm is up, pull to the right, resisting with the left arm, the elbow of your right arm describing an arc toward your right side. Try to pull the other arm up until you feel the stretch in your lat muscle, and pull back and forth in a slow, continuous pattern for twelve repetitions. Switch your hand positions after six reps.

OVERHEAD LAT PULL

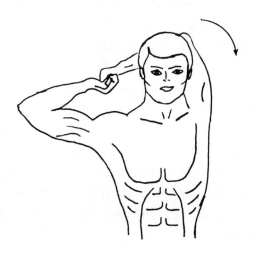

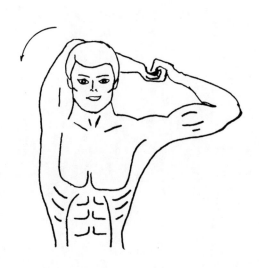

One-Arm Lat Head Pull

I mentioned in the chapter on neck exercises that pulling the head forward on the Forward Neck Pull also works the lats; it utilizes a compound movement by extension of the arm as it pulls the head forward and a slight downward pull like climbing. Using one arm at a time, some individuals can use this as a lat exercise.

I qualify this by using "some," as the exercise involves very strong neck muscles and not everyone will be able to use it. This exercise also has application in a workout routine as a dual movement at the end of the neck series and beginning of the back series, as it works both groups of muscles. The movement is similar to a Nautilus machine exercise for the lats. To perform this exercise, refer to the head pull and use one arm for the movement instead of two. Do six reps with each side.

ONE-ARM LAT HEAD PULL

PERSEVERANCE IS A SIGN OF WILL POWER

FROM: TAO TE CHING

124

Chapter Fourteen

Back - Lower

The lower back extends the body and aids in twisting the body from side to side. "To extend the body" means to straighten up from a bent over position. The muscles that lie along the spinal column are the ones involved. They start from the neck and extend down to the sacrum or tail bone. There are three primary groups of muscles, known collectively as the sacrospinalis muscles. Individually, they are the illocostalis muscles, laterally; the spinalis dorsi muscles, medially; and the longissimus muscles, in between the other two groups. The lower portion of these groups appears to be the most vulnerable to injury. Keeping the back strong and walking tall with good posture seems to be the most practical way of fighting our arch enemy, old age, and his henchman, gravity. Old age, and the sedentary life that insidiously comes with it, allows the back to become weak. Gravity starts to pull us over farther and farther into a leaning and hunching position, with our head bent in sort of a humbled bow. We allow old age to humiliate us, and when we bend over far enough, gravity goes for the headlock and the final throw, right into the wheelchair or bed.

An upright posture, on the other hand, uplifts our psyches and keeps us vital. Autotonics, as well as providing the *elixir vitae* for the whole body, has a couple of great exercises that strengthen the back and extend our lease on life—the first being the Bootstrap Pull.

Bootstrap Pull

This is a difficult exercise to perform for two reasons. First, it is hard to balance during the exercise because it requires using one leg as a resistor, and you must lift it off the floor. Second, the lift is done in three separate movements that eventually blend into one movement after you have learned the proper technique. You have to lean against the wall for balance when you begin the lift. Begin in a standing position with your shoulder against the wall, feet and legs together. Bend over and grab your leg behind the knee. Start with the leg that feels most comfortable to you to pick up from your leaning position. You begin with the knees in a locked position, and the first part of the lift consists of pulling the resisting knee forward into a bent position with the heel off the ground. This part really works the lower back if you resist hard enough with your leg. Next, lift the knee, using back strength, until you have completely straightened your back. From this position, you pull down with your leg, with your back resisting, until your toe touches the ground. The third part consists of locking the knee again, so the first and third parts resemble each other, but are opposite in action. After you learn the movement well, you should try to flow from one aspect to the next to form a single movement. Three reps with each leg to begin with will stretch and strengthen the lower back.

I like to call this lift pulling yourself up by your bootstraps, or the Bootstrap Pull. This is, of course, a cliche meaning to lift yourself out of a depressed state when you have sunk too far for your own good, thus uplifting your spirit. When you strengthen and straighten your back, you uplift your stature and your psyche.

BOOT STRAP PULL

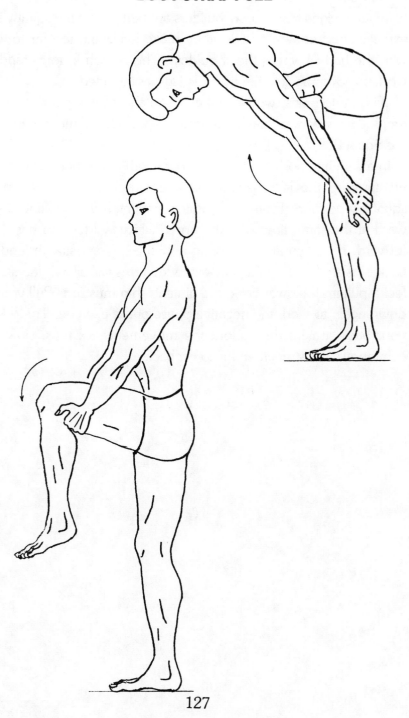

Squat Pull

When weightlifters or bodybuilders are performing the squat with barbell, one frequent mistake they make is leaning too far forwa with the barbell across the shoulders. This breach in form tends work the lower back rather than the legs, as intended.

With Autotonics, we can take advantage of this poor form ar employ it to work primarily the lower back, using a movement I c the Squat Pull.

In a standing position, feet shoulder width apart, bend over at t waist, grasp the legs behind the knees, and pull yourself into squatting position. From this position straighten up, resisting dow ward at the same time with the arms, which will tend to bend yc forward. If you continue resisting until the legs are straight and t back is as straight as your now-extended arms will allow, you shou feel a pull in the lower back and gluteals (hip muscles). Pull yours down again to work the negative phase of the exercise. Try to ke your back straight throughout the movement. Six reps, slow ar continuous, will strengthen the lower back.

SQUAT PULL

Seated Row

This is fun to do, and it works the back in the thoracic, lumbar, and sacral areas of the sacrospinalis group of spinal erector muscles. This exercise simulates a rowing machine, but the range of movement is about half. That is the half we want to concentrate on!

In a seated position, draw your feet up far enough so that you can grasp them with your hands. The grip is important here. Grip the foot from the outside below the ball and above the heel, along the edge. This gives a good grip for the hand and also places the most stress on the back as we do the movement. From this position, stretch the feet out in front as far as possible. This will pull your body forward and bend you at the waist. From this starting position, pull back, using your back muscles. As a result, your feet will be pulled toward you, and your knees will be drawn into your chest. Repeat the movement seven or eight times. You should feel a tiredness in your entire back.

SEATED ROW

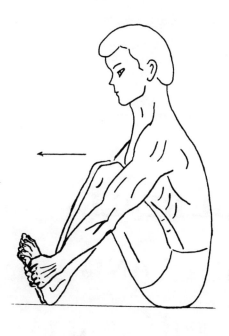

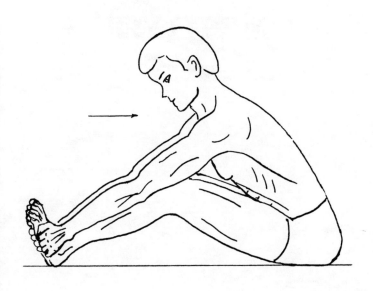

BE REALLY
WHOLE AND ALL
THINGS WILL
COME TO YOU

FROM: TAO TE CHING

Chapter Fifteen

Abdomen

This is my favorite group of exercises. Not suprisingly, this used to be the area I hated to work, but with the development of my innovative Autotonics movements, this is actually much more tolerable—sometimes even fun.

The abdominal muscles flex the vertibral column and aid in twisting the body. They are also the lie-detectors of bodybuilding. When the abdomen is slim and the muscles well-defined, you know you're in shape. When you've been cheating on your diet and drinking a little too much beer or pop, the belly tells on you right away. When you start to age, the "spare tire" that develops seems to be harbinger of a developing "blowout."

Beer belly, blubber gut, pot belly, battle of the bulge, love handles, spare tire, inner tube, fatso, doughboy, pot, cushion, pillow—call it as you see it, but you just can't hide it!

The first step in seeing any of your muscles is to rip off (bodybuilding lingo for diet) the fat, and recalling a few chapters back, you remember how this is accomplished—only be diet combined with exercise. Remember, I said "combined with," not separate. If you try to do it by exercise along, you end up looking skinny, gaunt, and tired. I think aerobics is good, but not as an overall fitness plan, and not as an obsession. If you try diet alone, I'm afraid you will end up looking about the same way, because the muscle tends to melt away while you are dieting, much faster than if you diet while you are working your muscles. Remember the old adage: Use it, or lose it.

There you have it. There is no way of circumventing it and coming up with a pleasing result. Let's assume that you are taking my little lecture to heart—how can we give these abdominal muscles nice definition when we finally get to see them and maybe even like the process?

I feel that I've developed, through Autotonics, the most unique set of abdominal exercises you have ever seen. In fact, I believe they are so unique that I'm going to take the liberty of naming them after myself. I will use my name to prefix each exercise to emphasize my contribution to the tummies of the world.

I will outline five new abdominal exercises, and you can judge for yourself how much fun they are.

The abdominal muscles are made up of flat sheets of muscle, interrupted by strong connective tissue. This is best seen in the rectus abdominis group that runs from the costal cartilages to the pubis. They are split into four distinct muscles on each side of the midline, stacked on each other like rows of bricks. Maybe this is where the term "built like a brick—house" comes from. Maybe.

Joining the rectus abdominis muscles on both sides are three layers of muscles arranged in different directions like the grain in wood, creating more strength and versatility of movement. They are, from the inside out, the transversus abdominis, whose fibers run in a perpendicular plane to the length of the body; next the internal abdominal obliques, whose fibers run oblique or slanted upward; and then the external abdominal obliques whose fibers cross in a downward fashion. This group of muscles aids in tilting and twisting the torso.

Farnham Standing Crunch

This first exercise, which I call the Farnham Standing Crunch, is a compound movement and may be difficult to understand from description. It's kind of like riding a bike—no matter how many instructions you receive, you only really know how after you've learned to ride.

To do the crunch, you have to think of yourself as not only bending over at the waist, but also contracting (crunching) your abdomen as tightly as you can.

The starting position is as follows. Place your legs wide apart, the

135

feet wider than shoulder width. Place your hands on your knees; this will bring you into a slight squat, bent at the waist. At this point tense your abdominal muscles—bend forward and down, shortening the abdominals, even drawing the pubis forward and upward. When you are fully crunched, you will be bent forward as if looking back between your legs, arms bent at the elbows. Don't lose this tension, but push yourself straight again with your arms, resisting all the way with the tense abdomen. At the top of the movement, keep the tension and crunch yourself down again. Continue for ten reps. Your arms, your chest, and your abdomen should all feel very worked.

FARNHAM STANDING CRUNCH

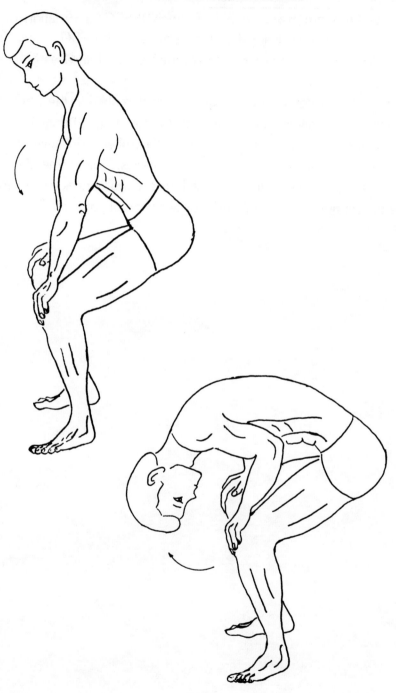

Farnham Standing Side Crunch

The Farnham Standing Side Crunch (FSSC. a variation of the FSC) can be done from the same stance as the FSC, except that you place both hands on one knee, the forward hand being the side you choose to start on.

You go through a similar sequence as described in the FSC. This movement involves an initial twist in the torso, so it brings into play the abdominal oblique muscles, too. Remember, you have to work both sides to balance your abdominal muscles. Don't forget the basic Autotonic precepts of slow (about four second contractions) movements, continuous tension, and concentration of your "chi."

FARNHAM STANDING SIDE CRUNCH

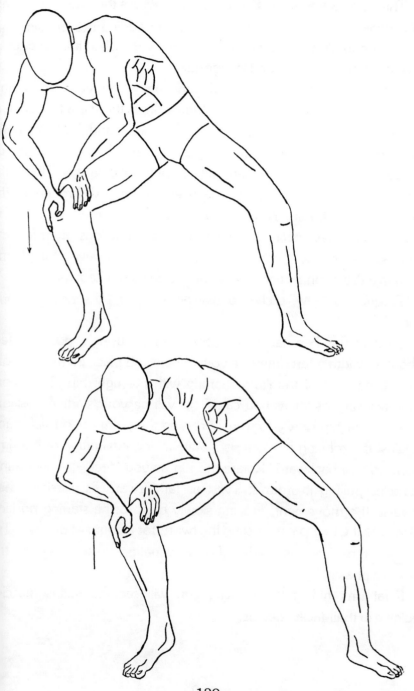

Farnham Twist

This next exercise, the Farnham Twist, works the abdominals with a completely new twist (pun intended). In addition to isolating on rectus group along with the side abdominal muscles, it inadvertently works the back serratus and intercostals.

You have to be careful, and concentrate on your abdominal muscles, making them do most of the work, as there is a tendency to drive the hip forward with too much gluteal and back strength. Remember, in Autotonics, the foundation is based on mind and body interaction, concentration, and isolation of muscle groups. That is the reason anatomical description has been so detailed throughout the course of the book. You should try to form a mental picture of how the muscles attach, and their anatomic functions, then feel the muscles as you go through the motions; the positive (Yang) and negative (Yin) contractions of the muscle being worked.

To quote a "new" cliche popular on a recent TV series: "It works for me."

Back to the Farnham Twist. Stand in an upright position, feet shoulder width apart. Interlace your fingers and place them over your hip at the crest of the ilium, starting with the right hip. Twist your hip backward as far as you can. This will be your starting position. Rotate your hip slowly forward, pressing the palm of your left hand against the rotating hip to resist, while taking advantage of the right hand to pull backward. Rotate the hip as you "feel" the abdominal muscles pulling it around. Twist as far forward as possible, then reverse the movement, twisting slowly back to the starting position (this time the rear palm resisting the twist), for a count of one rep. Try for six reps on each side. (For a variation, resist only in the positive phase.)

If fat isn't hiding the muscle, you will see the rectus muscles bulging in their facial sheaths.

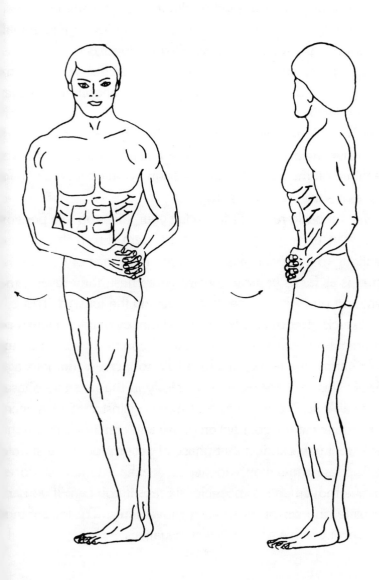

Farnham Knee Push

The previous group of exercises gives the top, middle, and side positions of our abdomen a good workout—now for the lower part of the rectus muscles. Your can't work out the lower abdominal without subsequently working the hip flexors, specifically the illacus, iliopsoas, and psoas muscles. The next two exercises will take care of those hip muscles at the same time as the abdomen, so they won't be included in a separate exercise.

The Farnham Knee Push is the first of the lower rectus exercises. This exercise can be done while lying on your back or with the back at an angle raised off the floor. The first position I would recommend for beginners, as it is the easier of the two.

Lying on your back, raised or flat, bring your knees up to a position so that you can place your hands against them. From this starting point, continue to flex your hips against the resistance of your arms. Flex your hips as far as you can toward your chest, then reverse the movement and push your knees back, keeping the tension. This is a very hard exercise to do, and you will find that even after a few reps your abdominal muscles will begin to tire. If you find yourself tiring, move your hands down your thighs a little to increase the leverage of your legs. This exercise works very nicely in the negative phase. When you can't flex your knees any more against arm resistance, relax the resistance in the contraction phase and continue to push the knees back until you exhaust that phase of action, too. You should try to carry these movements to negative exhaustion. First do as many positive movements as possible, six reps if you can. If you are able, complete one set of six positive movements. Try for another set of six, even if you have to finish with negatives.

FARNHAM KNEE PUSH

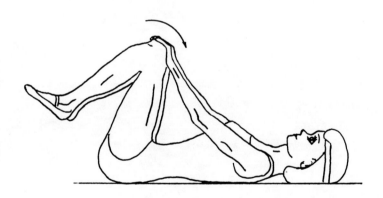

Farnham Seesaw

The last tummy tightening exercise, the Farnham Seesaw, is my personal favorite. You should do this on a rug, as it requires certain amount of friction between the floor and your body. You can create enough friction with your elbows and knees to perform the exercise, but if you can find a heavy or immovable object to grip, you can create more tension in your abdominal muscles.

The starting position resembles that of the Muslim paying homage to Allah. You are on the floor on your knees and forearms, head down between your arms, and your buttocks in the air. Grip your object, if available. The distance between the knees and elbows should allow you to seesaw yourself back and forth, about 10 inches. You should get a good stretch in your arms and lats on the backward phase of the movement. The backward movement brings into play the hip flexors and the lower abdominal muscles. In the forward phase, your lats pull and abdomen resists. Create the tension in your abdomen. Keep a slow pace, and very soon, after three or four reps, you will feel your rectus muscles fatiguing. You should be able to do six to twelve reps in this movement.

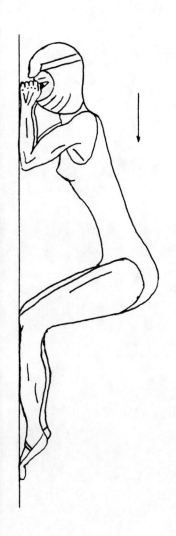

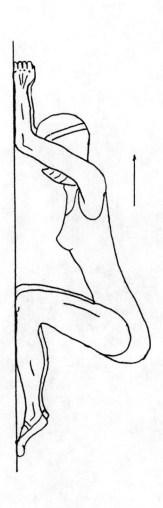

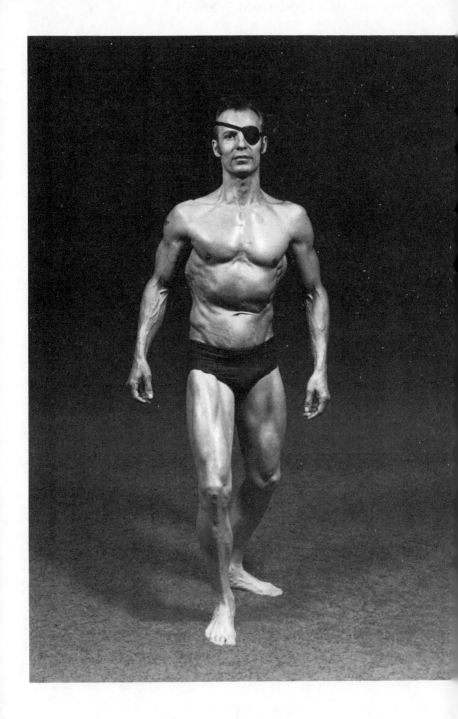

Hips and Legs

In most cases the limiting factor in the life of an athlete is his or her legs. Joe Namath's brilliant career was cut short because his knees couldn't hold up under the stress of the game. The most classic example is that of Muhammed Ali. When his legs started to slow, he started to get hit, and although I've never seen an athlete with more heart, his legs signaled his decline—several years before his courageous spirit gave way.

Athletes are striking examples of the importance of strong, youthful legs, and the example should underline the legs' importance to us ordinary people. Our onset of weakening legs is more insidious, but the conclusions we can infer will be the same. Too many armchair sports may very well lead us to early retirements. We should all try to "float like a butterfly, sting like a bee" for as long as we can.

Running or jogging is great for improving cardiovascular and respiratory functions, and probably should be included in any overall fitness program, but I feel that the disadvantages as a total fitness plan outweigh the advantages. First of all, the leg as it is exercised in running or jogging doesn't move through the full range of motion of flexion and extension, which is vital for the full development of the muscle. Jogging tends to build the quadriceps and lower back muscles at the expense of the hamstrings and abdominal muscles. Second, and most important, it causes a wide range of physical injuries because of the stress exerted on the joints, ligaments, and tendons as the foot hits the ground repeatedly, with <u>several times body weight</u> each time.

Jumping rope seems to have all the aerobic benefits, without the disadvantages, so it would seem to be a healthier alternative.

Autotonics, on the other hand, is an anaerobic exercise, but from the standpoint of building overall leg and hip strength and fitness, without the possibilities of physical injury, it is superior to any aerobic form of leg exercise.

The hip flexors have been discussed previously in conjunction with the abdominal exercises, but the hip, as a ball and socket joint, has a complete range of movement from flexion to extension, abduction to adduction, and a certain amount of rotation.

The major hip extensor is the gluteus maximus muscle or the buttock. Abduction of the hip and leg is performed by the gluteus medius and gluteus minimus muscles.

Adduction of the hip and leg is a function of the gracialis adductor longus, adductor brevis, adductor magnus, pectineus, and obturator externus muscles.

Rotation is accomplished by the gemelli, obturator externus, obturator internus, piriformis, and the guadratus fermoris muscles.

The gluteus maximus and other hip muscles are emphasized in many workout programs including mainly calisthenic movements and women seem to be drawn to them as though the magic elixir for smaller hips were contained in a certain number of leg extensions, kickouts, side thrusts, etc. If this were the answer, a person would be better off taking karate, with its emphasis on kicking techniques. She could kill two birds with one side kick, so to speak. She could learn to defend herself while she reduced the fat from her hips. This would certainly do more good, because an hour or so spent in the dojo would burn more fat than the five minutes spent on the gym floor going through the various hip movements.

Exercise is great and necessary, but it is not the way to reduce. Reducing the speed and frequency of the masseter muscles (jaw muscles used for chewing food) has a direct relationship to the glute area. The proper hip reducing formula can then be stated as Autotonics exercises - excess calories = sexy buttocks.

Gluteal Situp

This exercise works the buttocks extensor muscles through a full

148

ange of motion. As it works the buttocks it also works the back, arms, upper back, and lats, so the movement can be classified as a compound exercise.

Assume a sitting position on the floor, legs extended in front of you. Grasp one leg behind the knee, pull back on your leg, keeping it straight as you move to a lying position with your leg straight up. Keep pulling, bending your knee, until you pull your knee as close to your chest as possible. Try to flatten your shoulder into the floor. Now reverse the movement, pulling yourself back into sitting position again. Remember to resist hard on the reverse motion, so the buttocks receive a good workout, making sure you pull yourself up into a sitting position using the gluteal extensors. Avoid the temptation of using the momentum of swinging your leg.

This exercise isn't too hard to do and can be substituted for some of the harder back exercises for the beginner, as it works the back and buttocks. Try six reps with each leg as one set.

Because so many muscles are involved in the correct performance of this exercise, it could be included into an ultra-short workout. By combining the Gluteal Situp with the Farnham Seesaw, you can work most of the major muscles of the torso. Combining these two exercises works the hip flexors, hip extensors, torso flexors (abdominal muscles), torso extensors (sacrospinalis), arms (forearms and biceps), middle back (latissimus dorsi), and upper back (rear deltoids and rotater cuff group). If you add the Lunge for the legs (quadriceps and hamstrings), the Head Side to Side (neck, deltoids, and trapezius) and the Bent Press for the chest and triceps, you can provide exercise for the whole body in just five exercises. If time is your problem, but you're longing to get into better shape, try the "Autotonics Infallible Five," routine.

Even though 15-20 minutes of this routine gives you the best short exercise routine you can find, don't forget the Autotonics principles of slow, concentrated effort with equal emphasis on the Yin and Yang phases of the movement. Don't forget the meditative

reward you get while you're concentrating on your "chi," a goo
way to start or end a hard day.

GLUTEAL SITUP

Lunge

To firm up the buttocks area using Autotonics, the exercise choice is the Lunge.While strengthening the gluteal muscles, it also works the hamstrings, quadriceps, lats, and arms.

Assume a standing position, with one leg extended in front of the other with the knee bent so that the knee of the forward leg is over the foot, the back leg is extended, and the body is in a low front stance like a karate front stance. Bend forward and grasp the front leg behind the knee, pull forward with the arms and body, and simultaneously straighten the knee against this resistance. Continue the tension throughout the movement and after locking the knee pull yourself back into the Lunge stance. Continue slow tension movements of six reps with each leg. So much muscle is involved in these movements that you get very exhausted, but persevere and the benefits of the exercise will extend farther than your buttocks.

LUNGE

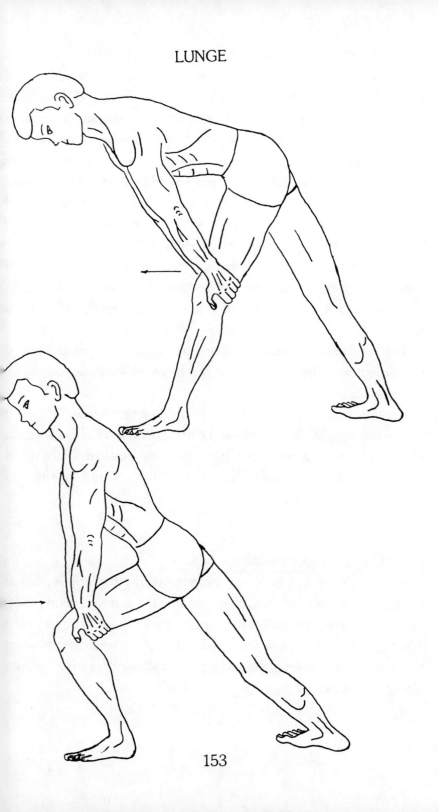

Seated Leg Laterals - elbows out

To work the abductors of the hip and leg, you have to sit on th
floor. The object of the exercise is to try to spread your knee
(abduction), while applying resistance with your shoulders, arms, an
pecs. This movement is very similar to one previously described fc
the chest (the Pec Squeeze), but in order to create more resistanc
for the legs, the movement has been modified. In a sitting positio
and with the knees bent and together, place your elbows on th
outside and against them. Squeezing your elbows together, sprea
your knees apart as far as you can, slowly, with controlled resistanc
Keeping constant tension, squeeze the knees together again. A
mentioned earlier, four seconds each way, positive and negativ
Open up your Chi force and let it flow. Six full reps should be dor
for a set.

The movement works the pectoralis major very strongly and th
movement can be used as a combination exercise, as will t
described later.

Another point to consider is that the pectoralis muscle may ti
before the legs, but the movement can be continued in the spreadir
phase. In other words, the legs are only resisted while in th
spreading phase, brought together, then spread again, un
exhausted.

Seated Leg Laterals - Variation

A variation of the previous exercise works the smaller rotatc
muscles along with the abductors. Assume the same position, excep
that when the knees are spread apart, the heels are kept togethe
this causes the leg to rotate laterally and brings the rotators into actioi
You may want to alternate exercises for variety and for fuller develor
ment of the area.

SEATED LEG LATERALS - ELBOWS OUT

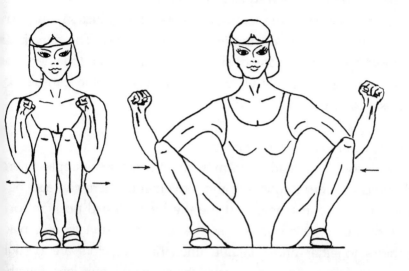

SEATED LEG LATERALS - VARIATION

Seated Leg Medials - elbows in

Adduction is the opposite of abduction, so in this exercise knee are spread apart and then squeezed together.

The basic position is the same as described for abduction, only now the elbows are placed on the inside of the knees. The exercise is started with the knees spread, slowly squeezing them together. This movement concomitantly works the rear deltoids and can also be used as a combination exercise.

Seated Leg Medials - Variation

A variation of the adduction movement can also be applied here with heels together throughout the movement. There can also be combination: for instance, start the the heels-spread position for count of four repetitions, and as the shoulders start to tire, place the heels together and continue until the adductors are brought to positive failure (you are unable to squeeze your legs together again). You can apply more force with your arms in the heels-together position because you can place your palms together, forming stronger resisting force to spread your knees.

SEATED LEG MEDIALS - ELBOWS IN

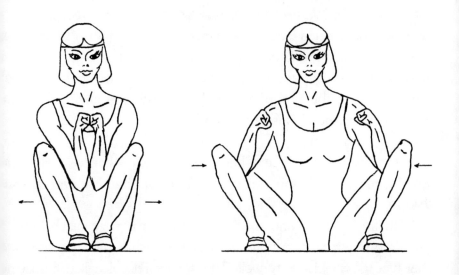

SEATED LEG MEDIALS - VARIATION

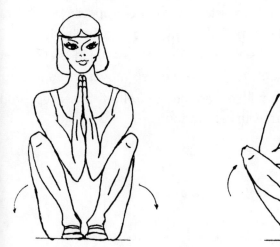

Lying Leg Extension

The quadriceps femoris is composed of the vastus medialis, vastus intermedius, and vastus lateralis muscles, as well as the rectus femoris muscle. These fibers blend together at the knee to form the patellar tendon in which the knee cap is incorporated. The pateller tendon attaches to the tibia, the large bone of the lower leg, or shin bone. Contraction of this group of muscles extends the knee joint. The rectus femoris muscle also acts as a hip flexor because it attaches to the ilium, or hip bone.

Extending the leg at the knee, against a resistance, builds the quadriceps group of muscles (the muscles on the front part of your thigh).

With free weights and machines you perform leg extensions to build the quadriceps. Autotonics uses two techniques that duplicate that type of exercise very well. The first exercise is called the Lying Leg Extension.

Begin by lying on the floor on your back. Bring your legs up to a perpendicular position, but bent at the knees. Hook one leg over the other at the ankle. Now slowly move the target leg into an extended position straight up, while resisting with the opposite leg. After reaching the top position, pull the target leg back slowly with a strong flexion of the resisting leg. The upper thigh stays fixed throughout the movement, and the lower leg moves through a full arc. If done slowly, with full concentration of effort, at six reps your thighs should start to burn with exhaustion.

LYING LEG EXTENSION

Rocking Horse

The second quadriceps exercise I call the Rocking Horse. This movement is shorter in range, and if done after the leg extensions (or supersetted), you can get a tremendous burn in the quadriceps. It can also be used alone as a variation exercise in your routine.

Begin the movement lying on your back in the same way as in the leg extension movement. Bring one leg up so you can grasp the ankle with your hands instead of using the other leg. The leg is now in an acutely flexed position against your chest. From this point, extend (straighten) the leg; this movement will bring your body into a siting position. Pull the leg back into flexion, which will bring you down on your back again. Rocking back and forth, using the quadriceps to generate the motion, brings the muscles to the boiling point very rapidly. Six good reps with each leg will prove you're not just horsing around.

ROCKING HORSE

Lying Leg Curl

The muscles in the back of the thigh are collectively called the hamstring muscles. They are composed of the biceps femoris, semi-membranosus, and semitendinosus muscles. They perform a dual function because of their attachments. They flex the knee and extend the hip as you experienced in the Lunge where they performed the dual action. We can also isolate them to flex the knee only.

This isolation hamstring exercise is called the Lying Leg Curl. To perform the exercise, lie face down with your legs extended. Hook one leg over the other at the ankle area and curl your leg toward your buttock as far as possible, resisting strongly with the opposite leg. Force the leg back down again, resisting, of course, for six to ten reps with each leg.

The foot position on this movement is important. If the toe is pointed back, ankle extended, the calf muscle relaxes during the movement, and the hamstrings do all the work of flexing the leg. If the toes are brought forward or the ankle flexed, the calf is tightened and will be involved during the exercise. This is one way to work the gastrocnemius muscle, and another way will be described later. Also, rotating the toes, inward puts more tension on the biceps femoris; rotating them outward puts more on the semitendinosus.

Another important point to consider is to raise the hips slightly before starting the movement; this creates more tension on the hamstrings. You can use a pillow to accomplish this, but you create a much better tension without it.

LYING LEG CURL

Lunging Toe Raise

The calf is probably the hardest muscle for Autotonics to exercise effectively because of the relative strength in the muscle and the inability to create an effective anatomic advantage to compensate for this strength. The calf is composed of the gastrocnemius muscle and the soleus muscle. The gastrocnemius attaches to the femur at one end, and through the Achilles tendon to the heel or calcaneus bone. Because of its attachment to the femur, it assists in knee flexion.

The soleus lies under gastrocnemius muscle and does not cross the knee joint. It inserts with the gastrocnemius to form the Achilles tendon.These muscles are called, collectively, the triceps surae. There are many more muscles in the lower leg that flex and extend the ankle and toes and rotate the foot. These assistor muscles that extend the ankle can be worked by pointing the toe in or out while performing the calf exercise.

To work the calf muscles, assume a Lunge stance, place your hands on top of the knee, getting your body weight as much over your lower leg as possible. From this position rise up on your toes to full extension. Remember to push back down again, don't let yourself just drop back. By placing a block under the ball of your foot to get a greater range of extension and flexion of the ankle, you can increase the effectiveness of the workload considerably. You can do many more reps with this exercise than with any previous exercise; therefore, I would suggest doing them to failure or to where the burn gets so bad that you have to quit. This usually takes twenty to twenty-five reps. You can try doing these after skipping rope to get more of a workout.

The main disadvantage from this position is that the knee is bent. This neutralizes the gastrocnemius muscle to a great extent; consequently, you must make sure that on the hamstring exercises you keep the ankle flexed to work the gastrocnemius.

This ends the chapters on the exercises.

LUNGING TOE RAISE

Epilogue on the Exercises

The preceding chapters represent a unique group of exercises that have been designed with the same logical theme that an exercise physiologist would use when collaborating with a design engineer to create an exercise machine.

Autotonics does not create a machine; it provides a logical system of exercises specifically designed to fit the machine that has already been created—"the ultimate exercise machine, your body."

PART FOUR

PUTTING IT TOGETHER
HOW TO
HOW MUCH
HOW OFTEN
GO FOR IT!

THIRTY SPOKES

SHARE THE WHEELS

HUB

IT IS THE CENTER

HOLE THAT MAKES

IT USEFUL

FROM: TAO TE CHING

Chapter Sixteen

How to, How Much, How Often

One of the biggest problems with any exercise program is proper direction. Most of the time you have to learn by trial and error, and even with the most expert guidance there are certain things that you find will work or not work in your personal case.

I will try, now that I have introduced you to Autotonics, to give you a method of approaching the exercises, depending on how much time you have to exercise and what your particular goals may be.

The exercises show you how to work your muscles. Now I will show you how to combine the exercises into a logical program to obtain a full workout.

First, you should try to envision your goals. Are they to tone up the muscles a bit? Or, perhaps a little more serious, to get back into reasonably good shape. Maybe to start bodybuilding and gain some of the principles before becoming a hard core iron pumper? The appeal of the varied advantages of Autotonics should convince you to try it and stay with it. If you're already into bodybuilding, you may want to use Autotonics for an auxiliary exercise method. If you're involved in another sport, you may want to choose a few exercises that might benefit your sport. Autotonics is versatile and adaptable; it can be used as a whole or in part, whatever your particular want or need.

Let's begin with the person who wants to tone up a bit, but doesn't have a lot of time to devote to exercising. For this person, taking advantage of the push and pull of opposing muscle groups will give a good workout with emphasis on a conservation of time. Keep in mind that although we're trying to conserve time, in every workout the goal should be to work out all the muscle groups. Ideally, they should be stressed enough to cause adaption and growth.

Another important point that must be mentioned before getting into the workout routines is proper pre-exercise warmup. You can use any method you like, such as twisting, stretching, or running in place. I like side bends and upper torso twists to warm up. You can also do Autotonics movements as warmups, by doing a set with moderate tension before doing a full tension set. Stretching and massaging your muscles after the workout ends or after each exercise will help prevent muscle soreness.

It is a good idea to stay warm while you work out, but avoid overheating. A warm shower or bath after a workout improves circulation, increases metabolism, and stimulates muscle growth.

The following workout routines are designed for a full workout. You must be sure to apply enough resistance to get a good workout. Remember, in any endeavor, it usually follows that the more you give, the more you get back: so, give it all you've got!

Routine One
Autotonics Infallible Five (15-20 minutes)

1.	Lunge	6 reps each leg
2.	Gluteal Situp	6 reps each leg
3.	Bent Press	6 reps
4.	Farnham Seesaw	6-10 reps
5.	Head Side to Side	6 reps each arm

This exercise should be performed at least three days weekly; e.g., Monday, Wednesday, Friday. Remember Autotonic principles and make this short routine worthwhile.

Routine Two
Combination Workout #1 (20-30 minutes)

1.	Lying Leg Extension	1 set, 6 reps each leg
2.	Lying Leg Curl	1 set, 6 reps each leg
3.	Seated Leg Medials-elbows in	1 set, 6 reps
4.	Head Side to Side	1 set, 6 reps each side
5.	High Pec Push	1 set, 10-12 reps
6.	Farnham Standing Crunch	1 set, 10-12 reps
7.	Bent Over Row	1 set, 6 reps each side
8.	Bootstrap Pull	1 set, 3 reps each side

Routine Three
Combination Workout #2 (20-30 minutes)

1.	Toe Raise	1 set, 10-20 reps each leg
2.	Lunge	1 set, 6 reps each leg
3.	Seated Leg Laterals-elbows out	1 set, 6 reps
4.	Knee Push	1 set, 6 reps
5.	Triceps Bent Press	1 set, 6 reps
6.	Lateral Shoulder Pull/High	

	Trap Pull Combo	1 set, 10-12 reps
7.	Cross Body Row	1 set, 6 reps each side
8.	Seated Row	1 set, 6 reps

Routine Four
Combination Workout #3 (20-30 minutes)

1.	Rocking Horse	1 set, 6 reps each leg
2.	Lying Leg Curl	1 set, 6 reps each leg
3.	Farnham Seesaw	1 set, 6-8 reps
4.	Cross Body Row	1 set, 6 reps each side
5.	Bent Press	1 set, 6 reps
6.	Medial Shoulder Rotation	1 set, 6 reps each arm
7.	Lateral Shoulder Rotation	1 set, 6 reps each arm
8.	Squat Pull	1 set, 6 reps

N.B.: These exercises can be varied throughout the week, Monday, Wednesday, and Friday, to give a more rounded development.

This second group of exercises I have designed for that person who has a little more time and wants a good program of overall body strength and fitness. This series of exercises emphasizes more specific concentration on body parts; although crossover muscle groups are used, the main emphasis is on the target muscle.

Routine Five
Overall Fitness Workout #1 (45-60 + minutes)

1.	Head Push	1 set, 6 reps
2.	Lateral Shoulder Raise	1 set, 6 reps each arm
3.	P.D. Pull	1 set, 10-12 reps
4.	Standing Shoulder Shrug	1 set, 6 reps each side
5.	Overhead Lateral Pull	1 set, 10-12 reps
6.	Bent Over Row	1 set, 6 reps each side
7.	Bracialis Curl	1 set, 6 reps each arm
8.	Forearm Curl	1 set, 6 reps each arm
9.	Long Head Triceps Extension	1 set, 6 reps each arm
10.	Farnham Standing Crunch	1 set, 6-10 reps
11.	Pec Push	1 set, 10-12 reps
12.	Low Pec Push	1 set, 10-12 reps
13.	Seated Leg Laterals-elbows out	1 set, 6 reps
14.	Lying Leg Extensions	1 set, 6 reps each leg
15.	Lying Leg Curl	1 set, 6 reps each leg
16.	Seated Row	1 set, 6-10 reps

Routine Six
Overall Fitness Workout #2 (45-60 + minutes)

1.	Head Side to Side	1 set, 6 reps each side
2.	High Trap Pull	1 set, 6 reps each side
3.	Front Shoulder Raise	1 set, 6 reps each side
4.	Lateral Shoulder Pull	1 set, 10-12 reps
5.	Lateral Shoulder Rotation	1 set, 6 reps each side

6.	Medial Shoulder Rotation	1 set, 6 reps each side
7.	Farnham Seesaw	1 set, 6-8 reps
8.	Cross Body Row	1 set, 6 reps each side
9.	Seated Curl	1 set, 3 reps each leg
10.	Forearm Extension	1 set, 6 reps each arm
11.	Lateral Head Triceps Extension	1 set, 6 reps each arm
12.	Bent Press	1 set, 6 reps
13.	Seated Leg Laterals- elbows out	1 set, 6 reps
14.	Seated Leg Medials- elbows in	1 set 6 reps
15.	Rocking Horse	1 set, 6 reps each leg
16.	Lying Leg Curl	1 set, 6 reps each leg
17.	Bootstrap Pull	1 set, 3-4 reps each side

Routine Seven
Overall Fitness Workout #3 (45-60 + minutes)

1.	Head Pull	1 set, 6 reps
2.	Overhead Lat Pull	1 set, 12 reps
3.	Bent Over Row	1 set, 6 reps each side
4.	Biceps Curl	1 set, 6 reps each arm
5.	Forearm Twist	1 set, 6 reps each hand position
6.	Medial Head Triceps Extension	1 set, 6 reps each arm
7.	Farnham Twist	1 set, 6 reps each side
8.	Bent Press	1 set, 6 reps
9.	High Pec Push	1 set, 10-12 reps
10.	Front Shoulder Raise	1 set, 6 reps each side
11.	Lateral Shoulder Raise	1 set, 6 reps each side
12.	P.D. Pull	1 set, 10-12 reps
13.	Seated Shrug	1 set, 3 reps each side

14.	Lunge	1 set, 6 reps each leg
15.	Lunging Toe Raise	1 set, 20-25 reps each leg
16.	Lying Leg Extension	1 set, 6 reps each leg
17.	Lying Leg Curl	1 set, 6 reps each leg
18.	Squat Pull	1 set, 6 reps

The preceding exercise programs can be very tiring and should be attempted only after four to six weeks of the combination workout routines. The length of the workout should take at least as much time as set forth in the text, or you may be doing the exercises too fast. Remember, slow, concentrated movements are the key to Autotonics. These are sample programs designed to work all the muscle groups. Deleting any of the movements or doing them out of sequence upsets the balance of the program.

If you find the routine too exhausting or too long to be done all at one time, you can split the routine into a morning and evening session. In order to avoid overtraining, you should wait forty-eight hours between sessions. Monday, Wednesday, and Friday seem to be the best sequence for rest periods as well as social schedules but if you're inclined you can continue at forty-eight hour intervals without breaking for the weekend. The outlined programs can be alternated on every workout, or continued for a week or more at a time. Substitution movements can be interjected into the routines if you find a specific exercise too difficult, but be sure to use a similar exercise from the same muscle group.

After you have been on the overall plan for three months, you may want to move up to a more concentrated program, The next series of routines will continue with the same exercises, but they will consist of several sets of each exercise. Specialized training such as supersets will also be listed.

You will notice that in most instances sets will be limited to two sets of six reps, or ten to twelve reps, depending on the particular movement. If you've read any bodybuilding magazines or books you will find many major bodybuilders going up to twenty sets for a particular body part. You have the option to do as many set as you wish with the Autotonics exercises, but I think you will find that if you do them with proper form in slow, controlled, and concentrated effort, they will be self-limiting. In other words, you probably won't get beyond two sets of six to ten reps of an

176

exercise, because your muscles will be too exhausted. Also, it takes about two hours to go through a routine with slow, concentrated effort; therefore, time will become a factor.

Routine Eight
The Three Day Split

This routine involves working solely the upper body hard on Monday. On Wednesday the upper body is worked with less intensity using fewer sets, in addition lower body exercises are introduced. Friday, you concentrate on the lower body exclusively. This routine allows workout of both upper and lower body areas twice a week with a forty-eight hour rest period between.

Monday

1.	Front Shoulder Raise	2 sets, 6 reps each arm
2.	Lateral Shoulder Raise	2 sets, 6 reps each arm
3.	P.D. Pull	2 sets, 10-12 reps
4.	High Pec Push	6 reps each
5.	Pec Push	" " " "
6.	Low Pec Push	" " " "

2 supersets (items 4–6)

7.	Farnham Standing Crunch	2 sets, 10-12 reps
8.	Long Head Triceps Extension	6 reps each arm
9.	Lateral Head Triceps Extension	" " " "
10.	Medial Head Triceps Extension	" " " "

2 supersets (items 8–10)

11.	Bracialis Curl	6 reps each arm
12.	Bracioradialis Curl	" " " "
13.	Seated Curl	" " " leg

2 supersets (items 11–13)

Wednesday

1.	Lateral Shoulder Pull	1 set, 10-12 reps
2.	Lateral Shoulder Rotation	1 set 6 reps each side
3.	Medial Shoulder Rotation	1 set, 6 reps each side
4.	High Pec Push	1 set, 10-12 reps
5.	Bent Press Wide Stance	1 set, 6-8 reps
6.	Triceps Bent Press	1 set, 6-8 reps
7.	Special Autotonics Curl	1 set, 6-8 reps each side
8.	Farnham Twist	1 set, 6-8 reps each side
9.	Squat Pull	1 set, 6 reps
10.	Standing Shoulder Shrug	1 set, 6-8 reps each side
11.	Overhead Lat Pull	1 set, 10-12 reps
12.	Lunge	1 set, 6 reps each side
13.	Lunging Toe Raise	1 set, 20-25 reps each side

Friday

1.	Overhead Lat Pull	2 sets, 10-12 reps	
2.	Cross Body Row	2 sets, 6 reps each side	
3.	Farnham Seesaw	2 sets, 6-8 reps	
4.	Seated Row	2 sets, 6-8 reps	
5.	Seated Shoulder Shrug	2 sets, 6 reps each side	
6.	Farnham Knee Push	2 sets, 6 reps	
7.	Lying Leg Curl	6 reps each leg	2 supersets
8.	Lunge	" " " "	
9.	Lying Leg Extension	6 reps each leg	2 supersets
10.	Rocking Horse	" " " "	

11. Seated Leg Laterals-
    elbows out   2 sets, 6 reps
12. Seated Leg
    Medials-elbows in   2 sets, 6 reps

The Four Day Split

The principle in this series is based on pre-exhaustion of muscle groups. This is similar to the system extolled by Mike Mentzer in his Heavy Duty System. Mike Mentzer is a world-class bodybuilder champion. He created a bodybuilding system based on the principle that a short, extreme effort was more productive than longer periods of lesser effort. The idea is to work a muscle using an isolated movement, then immediately do another exercise for that same muscle using a compound movement (involving helper muscles). This method brings the target muscle into total fatigue.

With this routine you work out four days a week, upper body one day, and lower body the next, with a rest day in between.

The Four Day Split

Monday

2 sets	1.	Front Shoulder Raise	6 reps each side
		going immediately to the	
	2.	High Pec Push	6 reps each side (No rest between)
2 sets	3.	Lateral Shoulder Raise	6 reps each side
		going immediately to the	
	4.	Lateral Shoulder Pull	6 reps each side (No rest between)
2 sets	5.	P.D. Pull	10-12 reps
		going immediately to the	
	6.	Lateral Shoulder Pull	10-12 reps (No rest between)

	7.	Pec Push	10-12 reps
2 sets		*going immediately to the*	
	8.	Bent Press Medium Stance	6 reps (No rest between)
	9.	Special Autotonics Curl	6 reps each side
2 sets		*going immediately to the*	
	10.	Bent Over Row	6 reps each side (No rest between)
	11.	Long Head Triceps Extension	6 reps each side
2 sets		*going immediately to the*	
	12.	Triceps Bent Press	6 reps (No rest between)
	13.	Knee Push	2 sets, 6 reps

The Four Day Split

Tuesday

	1.	Overhead Lat Pull	10-12 reps
2 sets		*going immediately to the*	
	2.	Cross Body Row	6 reps each side (No rest between)
	3.	Seated Row	2 sets, 6 reps
	4.	Standing Shoulder Shrug	6 reps each side
2 sets		*going immediately to the*	
	5.	Head Side to Side	6 reps each side (No rest between)
	6.	Farnham Standing Crunch	2 sets, 6 reps

	7.	Lying Leg Extension	6 reps each side
2 sets		*going immediately to the*	
	8.	Rocking Horse	6 reps each side (No rest between)
	9.	Lying Leg Curl	6 reps each side
2 sets		*going immediately to the*	
	10.	Lunge	6 reps each side (No rest between)

Wednesday would be a rest day, then Thrusday and Friday would be a repeat of Monday and Tuesday. You could substitute a different back exercise for the lower back if you wished. The same holds true for the abdominal exercises.

The foregoing are examples of more concentrated routines. If you wish to do more sets, or reps, than outlined, you can do them at your discretion. Remember, at all-out concentration this is extremely tiring and may lead to overtraining. If you feel tired all the time, have headaches, feel nervous or depressed, seem more prone to infections, or feel bored or lackadaisical about your workouts, you may be overtraining, and some time off or a switch of activities may be in order.

A question that may be asked relative to the exercises concerns proper breathing technique. I feel that too much attention paid to breath control takes away from performance of the exercise. There-fore, I would make the suggestion that you breathe "naturally," that is, as your body tells you. Take in as many breaths as you need during the course of the movements, and if you have to stop between to catch your breath, be sure to do so. One thing you should not do is hold your breath during the exercises; this causes a Valsalva effect that increases blood pressure and may be dangerous.

183

Let me mention some specialized bodybuilding techniques that ca be applied with Autotonics.

First, the type of movements you are doing naturally wi Autotonics are called concentration movements. They are slo controlled efforts allowing about four seconds of time for the positi contraction and an equal time for the negative contraction of t movement. You can add to the intensity of contraction at the pe of the positive movement if you hold the muscle in the contract position, "peak contraction," for a short pause before starting t negative contraction. This idea has been mentioned in previo chapters on the exercises. A similar technique done after the exerci is called an isotonic contraction. In this case as soon as you fini the last repitition, flex hard the muscle you have just worked o and hold that tension for 6 to 10 seconds. The extended contractic helps to keep tissue building conditions in the muscle a little long with less intense effort.

I like to close my eyes and feel the "chi" in the area. Focusi on the "chi" helps me to feel the muscle, an imagery that is need for mind muscle control. It also calms the breathing and provid the psychological well being that sets Autotonics apart from oth systems.

After you have worked your way up to the advanced routin you can try going beyond a specific number of reps to what called positive failure, the point at which you can't perform anotl positive contraction in the exercise. This should be your goal the more advanced training if you have already completed t mandatory six reps. To carry an exercise to an even more extrer effort, a technique called negative failure can be employed. T muscles are actually stronger in the negative phase of the contracti than in the positive phase. To take advantage of this, once you ha reached positive failure, continue the exercises only in the negati phase until you reach a point where you no longer have a strength to resist a negative contraction. This is called negat ilure. The technique should be employed sparingly and certainly ot on every workout, as overtraining will result very quickly, and ou will lose muscle instead of gain it. Use it to shock muscle owth when you seem to have reached a plateau.

Another bodybuilding technique that can be used with Autotonics called "burns." They are short, rapid movements used at the end of exercise after reaching positive failure. The muscle will start to urt while you are doing them, and the pain has the sensation of urning; hence, the term "burns." About ten short, fast repetitions ould start the muscle burning. Burns can also be used at the end negative failure and carried to the point where no more muscle ovement is even possible. This should be used <u>only</u> as a muscle ocker and with discretion. The burning sensation is caused by ck of oxygen, buildup of lactic acid, and muscle spasms.

Another technique that can be applied with Autotonics involves a orkout partner. When you have reached a state of positive failure, partner can provide the resistance for continuing the exercise, lowing you to do two or three more movements. What I mean "allowing" is providing enough resistance so the exercise can be erformed, but only with the most extreme effort. In this case, the artner becomes the sole resistance. This technique is called "forced ps."

Chapter Seventeen

Go For It

In this book I have provided the reader with a very good genera overview of the bodybuilding process, coupled with a uniqu approach to exercising. The exercises have been created utilizing m own experience with weight training methods over the past twenty eight years. The advice and training methods give the exercis community an alternative, less cumbersome, and less expensiv approach to exercise.

In the previous chapters I have outlined bodybuilding principle from a physical standpoint. Let me end this book with some of m bodybuilding philosophy.

Recently, I entered a bodybuilding contest, and the following day attended a seminar given by one of the guest posers, Bertil Fox, bodybuilder from England. Mr. Fox holds numerous titles and ha competed several times in the Mr. Olympia Contest. It is hard t believe the size of this man, not so much in height and weight, bu in the amount of muscle packed on his skeletal frame. Descriptio could only be accomplished metaphorically.

During Mr. Fox's seminar, he patiently answered questions an gave bodybuilding advice on diets, drugs, and exercises. He had wit him for sale some videos on the workout methods he used. Th weights he used were awesome, and in most cases he required th help of workout partners to perform the exercises. He talked an explained his techniques for over an hour, and I hung on every wore looking for some stimulus to urge my somewhat aging body into nev growth. During the course of the afternoon, one thing struck m more than all the rest of his advice—his approach to working out. H said that as he got psyched up for a training session, he looked at th weights as the enemy, and it was he against the weights. If h completed the sets and reps as scheduled, he felt that he had wo over the weights. Left unsaid, but implied, the contrary must also have been true. At times he must have felt as if he had lost to the weights.

I have read in many fitness magazines that other top bodybuilders have similar approaches. They attack the weights, get mad at the weights, or become "animal" with the weights. Now, this may work for some people, and I have been guilty of this attitude a time or two myself. However, while this behavior is generally believed to be a way of relieving tension and aggression, I tend to believe that it does more to <u>build</u> tension and aggression, as I have observed from my own experience.

If you approach Autotonics with a different, a positive, attitude, you will achieve greater success, perhaps not in building pure muscle, but in bodybuilding defined as total mental and physical fitness.

As you go through the exercises, close your eyes, and concentrate on the Yang and Yin energies flowing in and out of the muscle as it is being worked in the positive and negative phases. Feel the "Chi," the life force, building up in the muscle being worked. Doing this elevates a purely physical workout into a meditative experience. Concentration increases in the muscle being worked, you lose track of your breathing, and it becomes calmer, extraneous distractions are blocked out, and you become one with yourself. When you get through with your workout, you have a nice physical tiredness and a very relaxed mental state. You may even want to sit quietly after the workout while your breathing and heart rate return to normal and continue the meditative state for a few minutes longer.

Ponder the last words of Siddhartha Guatama, the "Buddha." As he lay on his deathbed, he reportedly said, "Decay is inherent in all compounded things; strive on with diligence."

Appendix

List of muscles

Neck

Trapezius
Scalenus anterior
Scalenus medius
Scalenus posterior
Spinalis capitis
Spinalis cervicis
Semispinalis capitis
Splenus capitis
Sternomastoid
Longus capitis
Longus cervicis
Longissimus capitis

Shoulder

Deltoid (anterior, medial,
posterior)
Subscapularis
Teres major
Teres minor
Supraspinatus
Infraspinatus

Arm - upper

Biceps brachii (long and short head)
Brachialis
Coracobrachialis
Triceps brachii (long, medial, and lateral head)

Forearm
Brachioradialis—connects with upper arm
Pronater teres—connects with upper arm
Twenty muscles that flex and extend fingers and rotate wrist

Chest
Pectoralis major
Pectoralis minor
Serratus anterior

Back - upper
Trapezius
Levator scapulae
Rhomboideus (minor and major)

Back - middle
Latissimus dorsi
Serratus posterior
Teres major

Back - lower
Quadratus lumborum

Back - sacrospinalis group
Ilio costalis dorsi
Ilio costalis lumborum
Longissimus dorsi
Spinalis dorsi

Hips
Gluteus (maximus, medius, minimus)
Iliopsoas
Psoas (major and minor)
Iliacus

Obturator (externus and internus)
Piriformis
Gemellus

Legs - upper
Gracilis
Pectineus
Adductor (longus, minimus, magnus)
Satorius
Rectus femoris
Vastus medialis
Vastus intermedius
Vastus lateralis
Biceps femoris
Semitendinosus
Semimembranosus

Legs - lower
Gastrocnemius
Soleus
Several muscles that flex and extend the toes

Abdomen
Rectus abdominis
Transversus abdominis
Obliquus abdominis externus
Obliquus abdominis internus

Anatomy Chart - Front View

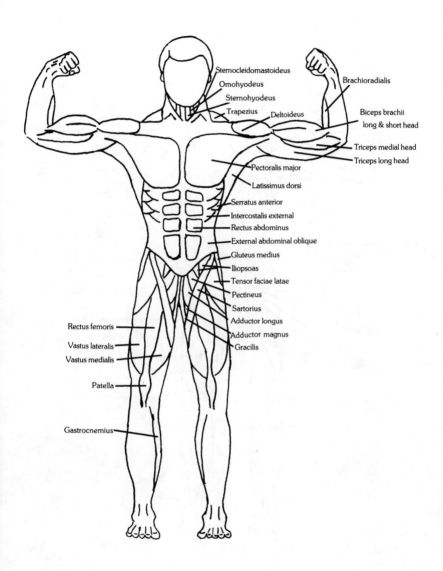

Sternocleidomastoideus
Omohyodeus
Sternohyodeus
Trapezius
Deltoideus
Brachioradialis
Biceps brachii long & short head
Triceps medial head
Triceps long head
Pectoralis major
Latissimus dorsi
Serratus anterior
Intercostalis external
Rectus abdominus
External abdominal oblique
Gluteus medius
Iliopsoas
Tensor faciae latae
Pectineus
Sartorius
Adductor longus
Adductor magnus
Gracilis
Rectus femoris
Vastus lateralis
Vastus medialis
Patella
Gastrocnemius

Anatomy Chart - Rear View

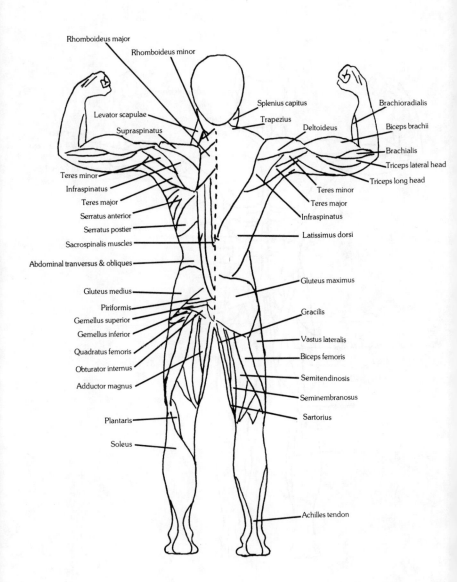

Rhomboideus major

Rhomboideus minor

Levator scapulae

Supraspinatus

Splenius capitus

Trapezius

Deltoideus

Brachioradialis

Biceps brachii

Brachialis

Triceps lateral head

Triceps long head

Teres minor

Infraspinatus

Teres major

Serratus anterior

Serratus postier

Sacrospinalis muscles

Abdominal tranversus & obliques

Teres minor

Teres major

Infraspinatus

Latissimus dorsi

Gluteus medius

Piriformis

Gemellus superior

Gemellus inferior

Quadratus femoris

Obturator internus

Adductor magnus

Gluteus maximus

Gracilis

Vastus lateralis

Biceps femoris

Semitendinosis

Seminembranosus

Sartorius

Plantaris

Soleus

Achilles tendon

Names of the Autotonics Exercises

Hips and Legs

Glossary

Abdominal - referring to the region of body from the bottom of the rib cage to the pubis. Bounded on the sides by the transversus abdominis, internal and external abdominal oblique muscles; in front by the rectus abdominis muscles.

Abduct - to move away from the median line of the body.

Abs - a bodybuilding term that usually refers to the rectus abdominis muscles.

Adduct - to move toward the median line of the body.

Anatomy - the study of the structure of the body and the relations of its parts. Anatomic - adj.

Autotonics - a unique approach to physical fitness that utilizes the opposing anatomical functions of the muscles to create a progressive and variable resistance exercise system, employing modern body-building techniques, mental imagery, and optionally—Eastern Philosophy.

Bench press - 1. a weight training exercise to work the chest muscles. 2. one of the three powerlifting contest lifts.

Bodybuilding - 1. a means of using progressive resistance exercises to build strength and muscle size. 2. increasing physical and mental well-being through exercise, diet, and healthful living.

Burns - a bodybuilding technique used at the end of a regular exercise movement, employing several more short, fast repetitions of the exercise until a burning sensation develops in the muscle.

This signals the release of lactic and pyruvic acids from stressed muscle cells. This type of stress leads to an adaptive increase in muscle size.

Cervical - refers to the neck region.

Chi - an undefinable energy that permeates the universe. The more it is concentrated, the denser and stronger the substance becomes.

Chins - a bodybuilding exercise that is performed by first hanging at arms length from a bar, then pulling yourself up, using arm and back strength until your chin touches or goes above the bar.

Compound exercises - in Autotonics, an exercise that works two groups of muscles at the same time with approximately equal resistance. 2. a bodybuilding term denoting the use of helper muscles to perform an exercise movement.

Crunch - a bodybuilding movement that emphasizes a strong contraction of the abdominal muscles, to tone and build the rectus abdominis muscles; employed in Autotonics in a unique form that gives the basic crunch movement increased intensity.

Curl - a bodybuilding exercise that builds the biceps and brachialis muscles by using weights or machine resistance in a curling movement; done in a similar movement with Autotonics, using opposing muscle strength for resistance.

Deadlift - an exercise and a competitive powerlifting movement that involves bending over to lift a barbell from the floor to a standing position. Tremendous poundages, close to eight hundred pounds, have been lifted in this manner.

Delts - a bodybuilding slang term that refers to the deltoid muscles that cap the shoulders.

ERN - an Autotonics acronym emphasizing how the triad of exercise, recuperation, and nutrition are elemental and inseparable in bodybuilding, physical fitness and sports in general

Extend - to straighten out.

Femur - thigh bone. Large bone in the upper leg.

Flex - to bend.

Flyes - a bodybuilding exercise that utilizes the anatomical function of the major chest muscles of flexing the shoulders. Different resistances are used, such as weights or machines to provide resistance against the arms as they are brought together in front of the chest. Autotonics utilizes body resistance for the basic exercise.

Forced reps - a term used to describe a method of assistance, usually provided by a partner, to gain a few more repetitions of an exercise, which increases the intensity of the exercise.

Front raise - an exercise used to build the anterior portion of the deltoid muscles. It involves raising the arm straight up in front of the body and using resistance to build the muscle.

Glutes - a slang bodybuilding term referring to the gluteal muscles, or the buttocks.

Hamstrings - a group of muscles in back of the thigh that flex the knee and extend the hip. The biceps femoris, semitendinosus, and semimembranosus muscles make up the group.

Humerus - the bone in the upper arm.

Ilium - the upper broad flat portion of the hip.

Ischium - the lower portion of the hip.

Isokinetic - moving a muscle through the full range of contraction and extension utilizing resistance.

Isolation exercise - an exercise that focuses on a single muscle or a portion of that muscle.

Isometric - contracting a muscle against resistance with no movement involved.

Isotonic - contracting a muscle with no resistance involved.

Joint - the area where two bones are joined, held together by ligaments.

Kinesiology - the study of anatomy as related to function.

Lateral - pertaining to the side.

Lateral raise - an exercise used to build the middle portion of the deltoid muscle by lifting the arm away from the side of the body and using resistance to build the muscle.

Lats - a slang bodybuilding term referring to the latissumus dorsi muscle, the broad muscle of the back.

Ligaments - strong fibrous tissue that hold bones together at the joints.

Lumbar - referring to the lower portion of the back.

Medial - referring to the middle.

Negative contraction - the lengthening phase of a muscle in a body-building exercise.

Negative failure - the inability to perform another repetition in the lengthening phase of an exercise movement because of muscle fatigue.

Overtraining - a term that denotes physical training carried to extremes, not allowing sufficient time for muscle recuperation, resulting in deleterious mental and physical manifestations.

Peak contractions - a technique that employs a deliberate, concentrated contraction held for a short pause at the end of the positive contraction phase of an exercise movement.

Pelvis - the area bounded by the hip bones.

Positive contraction - the shortening phase of a muscle in a bodybuilding exercise.

Positive failure - inability to perform another repetition in the positive contraction phase of an exercise movement because of muscle fatigue.

Pre-exhaustion - a bodybuilding technique that involves performing an isolation movement to tire a muscle, followed by a compound movement.

Pronate - turn the hand so the palm faces down or back.

Pubis - the hip bone forming the front of the pelvis.

Pump - a slang bodybuilding term referring to the swelling that occurs in a muscle during exercise because of increased blood circulation in the muscle.

Pump iron - to bodybuild using weights and ancillary equipment.

Pecs - a slang bodybuilding term referring to the pectoralis major muscles, the large chest muscles.

Radius - a bone in the forearm that serves as an attachment for the biceps muscle.

Reps - a slang bodybuilding term referring to repetitions, repeated actions in an exercise.

Rotate - twist on the long axis.

Row - a bodybuilding exercise that works the latissumus dorsi muscle through its anatomic function of extending the arm; e.g., movement used in rowing a boat.

Routine - a bodybuilding term describing a series of exercises done in a sequence.

Sacral - referring to the area in the lower back that forms the rear boundary of the pelvis.

Scapula - the large flat bone of the back, sometimes referred to as the shoulder blade.

Set - a specific number of repetitions of an exercise.

Squats - an exercise and a competitive powerlifting movement that is executed by doing a knee bend with a barbell across the shoulders. The movement is usually carried to a point where the hip joint is at a point below parallel with the knee.

Sternum - the cartilaginous structure that connects the ribs in front of the chest, sometimes referred to as the breast bone.

Supersets - several sets of related exercises performed with minimal or no rest between sets.

Supinate - turn the hand so the palm faces up or forward.

Split routine - splitting an exercise routine into two or more sessions to more effectively group exercises, conserve time, reduce strain, and circumvent overtraining.

Tendon - strong fibrous tissues that connect muscles to bones.

Tibia - the large bone in the lower portion of the leg, sometimes referred to as the shin bone.

Thoracic - referring to the area of the body enclosed by the ribs.

Tao - the way of nature; the ultimate undefinable reality.

Traps - a slang bodybuilding term referring to the trapezius muscles.

Tri-set - a series of three sets of related exercises performed with minimal or no rest between sets.

Ulna - bone of the forearm that serves as an attachment for the triceps muscle.

Vertebra - one of the bones of the spinal column. P1. vertebrae.

Workout - an exercise routine.

Yang - In Chinese philosophy, the forces represented by the positive, strong, male creative power, etc. It is never ultimate but always relative to the Yin.

Yin - In Chinese philosophy, the forces represented by negative, yielding, female, receptive power, etc. It is never ultimate but always relative to the Yang.

Order Form

Aardvark Books
Box 469-A
Hibbing, MN 55746

Name: _____

Address: _____

_____Zip:_____

Please send me _____ copies of Autotonics $10.95 each.

Minnesota residents please add 66¢ sales tax per copy.

Shipping: $1.50 for the first book and 50¢ for each additional book.

I understand that I may return this book for a full refund if not satisfied.

Order Form

Aardvark Books
Box 469-A
Hibbing, MN 55746

Name: _____
Address: _____
_____Zip:_____

Please send me _____ copies of Autotonics $10.95 each.

Minnesota residents please add 66¢ sales tax per copy.

Shipping: $1.50 for the first book and 50¢ for each additional book.

I understand that I may return this book for a full refund if not satisfied.